PROOF
COPY

Being Good At Being Bad

Troubled Teenagers: Factors and Solutions

By José Rosado

Edited by Pat Russo

Copyright © 2007 by José Rosado

ISBN 0-7414-4248-5

Published by:

INFINITY
PUBLISHING.COM

1094 New DeHaven Street, Suite 100
West Conshohocken, PA 19428-2713
Info@buybooksontheweb.com
www.buybooksontheweb.com
Toll-free (877) BUY BOOK
Local Phone (610) 941-9999
Fax (610) 941-9959

Printed in the United States of America

Printed on Recycled Paper

Published September 2007

Dedication

The dedication of this book is about offering appreciation and hope.

First, appreciation for those people closest to me who have been instrumental in my life and provided me with the unconditional support, encouragement and structure required to help me overcome my personal flaws and faults – my mother Rosa, my mentor Iris Cintron and my wife Margarita. These three women each had a hand in molding me into the man I am today.

My appreciation also extends to my two brothers – Juan and David – my companions through childhood and adolescence. They have both continued to be a source of strength and pride for me. The experiences that carried us through our turbulent youth now serve to bond us stronger than ever.

My offer of hope is for my children and grandchildren. My wife and I were blessed with three beautiful children – José Jr., Naomi Marie and Germain Stuart. As parents we have been diligent in our efforts to prepare our children for the real world and all that it has to offer – both good and bad. As they now venture out as young adults, I hope that the world is good to them and, likewise, that they will offer some good in return. God bless my babies; I'm very proud of them.

As a grandparent, my hope also extends to my grandchildren. Naomi and her husband Karim have been blessed and have blessed our family with two precious babies – Karim Nimar Brice Jr., and Gianna Chantel Brice. I want that their laughter bring smiles to others, that their tears be tears of joy and that they have the desire and ambition to pursue their dreams and goals and the compassion to help others do the same.

Foreword

There seems to be no end to the troubling facts regarding today's youth:

- A serious disciplinary action – including a suspension of five or more days, expulsion or a transfer to a specialized school – occurred in 46% of schools during the 2003-2004 school year. Approximately 655,700 such actions were taken nationally.

- Within a thirty-day span, 18.5% of high school students carried a weapon, 43.3% drank alcohol, 20.2% used marijuana and 2.1% injected an illegal drug[1].

- Almost 30% of our municipalities are experiencing gang problems[2].

- Within these areas, there are approximately 24,000 gangs with a membership of 760,000.

- In 2005, 24 percent of students ages 12–18 reported that there were gangs at their schools including suburban (21 percent) and rural (16 percent) students.

Noting these figures cannot fully capture the human, social and financial costs that the statistics describe. No amount of data can express the anger, pain and despair felt by the individuals, families and communities who have agonized over these concrete realities. While trends reveal important improvements over the past five years, it remains clear that there are many bad and tragically sad things happening to today's youth. These unwanted behaviors are particularly problematic among poor and minority youth. Indeed, far too many young people are becoming successful at Being Good at Being Bad.

José Rosado has devoted his career as an educator to dealing with these teenagers. His writing bears witness to the conditions that lead to the troubled lives about which he writes. He does not base his thoughts on an academic inventory of specific policy programs. Instead, Mr. Rosado's commentaries include specific and concrete ideas on what can be done. He frames his compelling case using his own life, the challenges he knew all too well while growing up, and his experiences as a school counselor and administrator. The book serves an important purpose with its clear description of the crucial interaction of family, school, popular culture and commerce in setting up children to live at risk of failure.

What makes this book so compelling and different is that Mr. Rosado confronts these risks as an issue of personal responsibility, not merely as social and economic issues. He asks us to recognize that economic deprivation, racism, corporate marketing, drugs and crime contribute to the widespread experience of dysfunctional families. He points to a popular culture that confronts marginalization by legitimizing the very behaviors that are putting teenagers at risk of self-destruction in their search for self-esteem and respect. Without constructive outlets in which to pursue this search, "being bad" becomes the basis for identity in school and in the neighborhood.

Yet the message of the book is not confined to blaming the system or blaming the victim. It recognizes and stresses responsibility and accountability by all – by the young people who become good at being bad in an attempt to establish a level of status, by those who judge and prejudge at-risk youth as not capable or deserving, and by those who are in a position to reach out by modeling success or by mentoring those in need of support. Individuals in a position to help need to accept responsibility to do so; individuals embracing a "thug" lifestyle in pursuit of respect from others need to accept the discipline and self-respect required to abandon the paths to being bad. As Mr. Rosado so passionately states,

> Many times, I wonder whether or not I am losing my sanity, but I believe that the irresponsible act of "going crazy" – lashing out in a destructive, reckless and violent manner with no regard for myself or others – in order not to have to face up to the mess that I have created in my own life, is no solution for me. (p. 23)

Indeed, Mr. Rosado concludes his chapter "Fear of Failure" by counseling that often "... the most difficult obstacles to overcome are those you place in front of yourself." (p. 153)

It is worth stressing that this book calls on everyone to believe that there is a better way. Most importantly, those who confront the gauntlet of at-risk behaviors should understand that the promise of a better life lies in the strength and discipline to refuse to give in to those things that will destroy their own health and well-being. Those who would succeed at Being Good at Being Bad still have some chance to break the cycle of discouraged lives and on-going poverty. This is a daunting task, however, and no child or adolescent facing the combination of problems described by Mr. Rosado can be expected to do this on his or her own.

Individuals – teachers, lawmakers, celebrities, parents and others – who are in a position to help but often do harm, despite their intentions, need to recognize when they do so. For those of us who are advantaged, we have a moral obligation to act accordingly. Organizing and supporting school or community youth-development programs might be part of this. It might involve reforms in the juvenile- and criminal-justice systems. Whatever we do, it will require the improved understanding and combined effectiveness of both parents and teachers. It will certainly involve public policies that support families, provide for the health and nutrition of children, and expand opportunities for meaningful employment and livable wages. It will also require an honest and open-minded consideration of the ideas presented in this book.

Some readers will find Mr. Rosado's proposals controversial. Those on the left might balk at his comments on freedom of expression in popular culture. They might feel his stories about welfare fraud and parental responsibility place the emphasis on the wrong issues. While conservatives might welcome such discussions, they might well have their own difficulties with his indictment of the role of profit making and commercial market activities. They might shrink from his arguments about changes in the drug laws. But let no one misunderstand the place from where these ideas emanate.

This book is a personal testimony, one that is informed by an understanding of the dynamics of being "bad" built on both personal and professional experience. One can hope that those who actually are at-risk will read this book. If they do, they will find a direct and accessible work. For the rest of us, there is an invitation to confront our own values and lifestyles, the opportunity to ask if we have been hypocritical or to evaluate how we have failed to seize the opportunity to change the imperatives of Being Good at Being Bad. For his part, José Rosado has dedicated himself to that task.

John V. Reynolds, Ph.D.
Professor of Political Science, Moravian College
Chairperson, Children's Coalition of the Lehigh Valley

CONTENTS

"...We're living a really fast life. The ones who have children, sometimes we don't have time to see them much. We come back from work; our kids are in bed already. We go back to work, out kids are off to school. We hear a great deal about kids today, how bad some are and that our American youth is rapidly deteriorating.

I think we can do something about solving our mounting difficulties at home. There is nothing wrong with our homes, our country, that a little more care, a little more concern, a little more love, won't cure. We need to show love and to love, not only our kids and our family as a whole but also our neighbors. We're all brothers and sisters, and we must give each other a helping hand when it is needed."

Roberto Clemente

"Each time I look at my children, I can say to them...whatever the obstacle...there's a chance for you. A chance for you to do whatever you want...to become whatever you want to become...and this chance exists so long as our free society exists."

Jackie Robinson

"To me, there are three things we all should do every day. We should do this every day of our lives. Number one is laugh. You should laugh every day. Number two is think. You should spend some time in thought. Number three is, you should have your emotions moved to tears, could be happiness or joy. But think about it. If you laugh, you think, and you cry, that's a full day. That's a heck of a day. You do that seven days a week, you're going to have something special."

Jim Valvano

Introduction

Understanding where I'm coming from on the issues will be easier if you understand where I've come from in life.

As you'll see from a brief autobiography that I wrote in 1989 while a graduate student at Lehigh University, I've lived through and survived many of the factors that contribute to the detrimental behavior of troubled teenagers – many times in spite of myself. Presenting my own life experience sets the stage for the issues that I'll address and the solutions that I'll propose in these pages. In each section, I've also included many real-life encounters from my personal and professional experience to provide additional perspective and insight on the issues.

Being Good at Being Bad is a lifestyle, one that's fostered by the experiences of failure in three critical areas: home, community and school. As children develop into adolescents and teenagers, encountering continued hardships in any of these three areas is the equivalent of a "strike" against them. When troubled teenagers "strike out" in these crucial areas, they adopt a being-good-at-being-bad attitude in order to strike back.

As illustrated by the quotes that open this book, it's vital that we pay more attention and demonstrate more affection in our efforts to redirect troubled teens. Our society presents ample opportunities for our children to overcome obstacles and experience success. However, making this a reality for many troubled teenagers requires a hard look at the many factors that contribute to these hardships. It will take the concerted effort of parents, educators, clergy, community leaders and elected representatives to minimize the barriers they face and maximize the potential opportunities.

It's my hope that this information will engage you at many levels. I hope that you'll laugh. I hope that you'll spend time in thoughtful debate over the factors explained and the solutions proposed. I also hope that you'll be moved – moved to tears and moved into action.

It's my intention to be very direct and to the point, without any long-winded rhetoric. As you read through the different sections of this book, ask yourself who profits from the many factors that contribute to the detriment of our young people. Who profits by assuring that the poor and uneducated remain poor and uneducated? Who profits by maintaining a prison population in excess of two million people in America? Who profits from the over identification of our children as "disabled?" Who profits when troubled teens become wards of the court, are labeled delinquent and incorrigible and are placed in private residential education/treatment facilities? Who profits when teens become addicted to drugs and alcohol?

Want to know who profits from the detriment of our young people? The policy makers, that's who. If you think this a stretch, consider this. As the two leading candidates for the 2008 Democratic Presidential nomination diligently worked to fill their campaign coffers, both Hillary Clinton and Barack Obama took close to one million dollars each from fundraisers hosted by record producers responsible for promoting rap artists and gangsta rap. This same music genre promotes violence, gangs, drug and alcohol abuse, the degradation of women and the use of the "n-word." These fundraisers took place a few months after the Michael Richards' "n-word" tirade and just a few weeks before Imus' offensive remarks regarding the Rutgers University women's basketball team. Other segments of corporate America also contribute tens of millions of dollars to presidential candidates, as well as for candidates for the U.S. Senate and Congress, along with candidates for state and municipal offices. Republicans and Democrats alike benefit from the profits of corporate America – even when it comes at the detriment of our young people. Did you think these types of campaign contributions came without strings? Continue to ponder this question as you read through this book.

If I'm successful in delivering the messages of *Being Good at Being Bad*, you'll have the insights necessary to make a positive difference in the lives of our troubled teens. Together, we will make this self-limiting behavior less common among our young people.

Section I

I Feel Ya'

Free at Last – No Longer Awaiting Enlightenment

It all makes sense to me now. Despite this knowledge, at times I still feel cheated. I still find myself asking, "Why me?"

Looking back, I see that I've come a long way from the rat- and roach-infested housing projects where I was raised, together with my older and younger brothers, our caring mother and our alcoholic father. The early stages of my pilgrimage led me through the Bethlehem Area School District, the same educational system where I'm now employed as a school counselor. Many of the people that I grew up with laugh at this and say, "You're a counselor?!"

I also question how this happened, but that's not because I question my qualifications. I'm a very competent and capable counselor, primarily because I've been able to survive a pilgrimage full of negative experiences. Because of that, I have a responsibility to offer guidance to others. Somehow, I've been able to endure because I've always known that, "All the truly important battles are waged within the self."[1] At any point, I could have easily made excuses and convinced myself that I couldn't succeed.

At every stage of my life, I've paused and asked myself, "Is this all worth it?" I once believed that I'd been given a raw deal because I grew up in the projects, in a neighborhood where the junkies shot up and littered the streets and parks with their dirty needles. I was a product of the welfare system, part of a family that waited for the food stamps to arrive so that mom could go grocery shopping. While we waited for the welfare check, my brothers and I hoped that we might get new sneakers.

Mom so wanted my brothers and me to graduate from high school, telling us that an education could change things. Today, I have a bachelor's degree, am working towards my master's degree, have a good career, and live in my own home together with my wife and children. Big improvement, right? Then why do I often feel that I was better off back in the projects, where I watched the rats and roaches running by in the hallway? I now believe that I have the answer.

Like many people, I've always thought that my life would improve once I achieved a certain goal. Graduating from high school was supposed to be the answer; it meant that I could get a job, make some money and start living a good life. Wrong! Flipping burgers just wasn't making it. So, one year after graduating from high school, off I went to college, where I encountered a new set of struggles. Again, I thought if I could meet the challenge, fulfillment would certainly be within my grasp. When it failed to materialize, I set off to graduate school. In the meantime, I got married and started a family. Later, I bought a home. Still, "The American Dream" didn't seem to be all that it was cracked up to be.

I now accept my struggle with a clearer vision. I've learned to accept my pilgrimage, knowing that, "Each accomplishment, itself, becomes the next obstacle to be overcome." [2] From this perspective, it becomes easier to accept my struggles and to avoid asking those unproductive "Why me?" questions.

These days, I'm pleased to have the opportunity to share my story. That's because I now understand that, "The telling of the tale will itself yield good counsel."[3]

Early Years of Happiness and Desire

Fun and laughter filled most of my childhood days. There were always kids to play with all day long. We enjoyed playing baseball in the park during the day, and ball tag, buck-buck, or kick the can at night. The same group was together day in and day out, only splitting up long enough to run home and eat.

Hot summer days meant racing down the wooded path to the city pool, where we'd sneak in by crawling under the fence, climbing over the bathroom wall, or by simply running past the attendant at the front desk. When the lifeguard whistled for us to stop running around the pool, and restricted us to the bench for a short time, even that was part of the fun.

I was very happy during this stage of my pilgrimage; maybe that's because I didn't know I was on one. I was under the impression that I was living the same type of life that most people lived. Even school was fun, as I walked to and from school with the gang. Things at home remained steady, as pop's drinking had not yet become an obvious problem. Nothing seemed to dampen my happiness, even though I often had to put cardboard in my sneakers to cover the holes and frequently used socks as gloves during the winter. We enjoyed the snow, as the gang would get together to take turns riding sleds and other objects down the big hill.

During this period, I experienced my first feelings of affection for a female. I can still remember her long black hair and her baby-blue eyes. Her name was Mary Lou. We considered her one of the guys, but this tomboy was also a sweet and very pretty girl. When we were in fifth grade, I sent her a big Valentine's Day card, hoping that it would communicate how much I really liked her. Instead, she saw it as a friendly gesture. It hurt me when she began liking other boys. I continued to drop hints about the way I felt about her, but she continued to treat me as a sweet and innocent friend. So instead, I acted as her protector, giving her piggyback rides and watching out for her when we would be out with the gang in our huts in the woods. There were numerous occasions when the two of us were all alone, but I could never summon up the courage to ask her out. I continued to watch her date other people. Even thought most of the guys she dated were my friends, I never though that they were good enough for her.

This internal struggle continued over the years. Deep inside of me, I had an empty, helpless feeling because she did not, or would not, respond to my endless efforts to make her understand my true motives. As I look back on this relationship, I can understand that "helpless as we are as children, to change the world, or to move on and take care of ourselves, we must develop ways of pretending that we are not so powerless."[4] What bothered me the most about the relationship was that everyone in the neighborhood knew how I felt about her. She must have known! Could it be that she was just as scared as me? That's probably so.

I remember the day that her family moved out of the neighborhood. I thought to myself, "There she goes and you never told her how you feel about her." It was as though I had lost her forever. Recalling these feelings now, I'm still confused over my silent debate about whether or not I was losing her. How could I lose something that I didn't have? Taking it a step further, what exactly did I have? Could it be that maybe I didn't lose out? Maybe I actually triumphed from establishing a good relationship with the object of my desire? But how good could that relationship have been? After all, I was afraid to tell her how I really felt.

Over the years, these questions raced through my mind every time I saw or thought about her. To this day, I still feel like that insecure little boy when I see her. It seems foolish to admit that I've felt this way ever since I've known her. I take comfort in knowing that "men have always tried to maintain illusions to protect themselves from living with the anguish of their unimportant momentary existence and their helplessness to change the absurdity of their needless suffering."[5]

It's useless for me to continue to torture myself with this "what-if thinking." By cherishing the memories and understanding the relationship that we had, couldn't I now put an end to this suffering and these childhood memories? Unfortunately, the answer is a resounding "No," as I discovered recently when our paths crossed at a local nightclub. There she was, as pretty as ever, talking with friends. I found myself rapidly approached her, which was not my normal reaction, but it had been such a long time since I'd seen her and I'd already had a few drinks in me. Despite my initial bravery, I was immediately transported back to my early insecurities when she saw me. "Oh my baby," she said as she smiled and grabbed onto my arm. The next thing I knew, we were on the dance floor.

Closing time arrived all too quickly. I found myself thinking, "She is gong to be leaving me again." There was no doubt in my mind that I had to tell her how I felt. A friend once told me, "The messenger doesn't rest until the message is delivered." I knew that the time to deliver the message about how I'd felt had come. She wasn't surprised to hear me confess that I'd always liked her and still thought about her often. For a few moments, we strolled together down memory lane. It was as though we again became those two little kids back in the South Terrace Housing Projects. The only difference was that now we were both a bit tipsy.

We walked together for a while, talking and enjoying each other's company, but the changes that had taken place in our lives were obvious. We had both married someone else and now had families of our own.

Relief finally set in when I told her how I'd always felt, but I guess it was a little too late for us. She will always live in my thoughts and heart. Although I understand the relationship now, there remains a feeling of emptiness within me. Having been enlightened, I can now deal with this feeling.

Adolescent Challenges

During my adolescent years, I began to notice that there were many differences in the way people lived and approached life. It was also at this stage of my pilgrimage that I really began to struggle.

My physical appearance began to change for the worse. Having always been a chubby kid, I could deal with my weight problem but then came the zits, which covered my face from my forehead, extending over my chin and down my neck. If that were not enough, I began growing breasts large enough to comfortably fill a girl's training bra. I confess that I never felt comfortable about my appearance during my adolescence. This may be part of the reason that I had so much anger within me.

Another factor that contributed to my increasingly angry demeanor was my home life. As pop's drinking became a more serious problem, yelling, screaming and arguing became a way of life at home. Fighting outside the home also became a way of life for me; no real reason was needed. A very happy child had been transformed into an angry teenager. I also began to realize that not everyone lived the same sort of life that I did. The hot summer days now meant picking tomatoes in the tomato fields or pushing a broom at the playground so that I could earn enough money to buy my school clothes.

Drugs had already become a part of my life by this time. I first smoked marijuana at the age of eight, when my uncle died in a tragic car accident and my older cousin started smoking pot to cope with his father's death. Like most of my friends, I learned that drugs could relieve our discomforts. By age 12, most of us were smoking pot on a regular basis. Some of my peers even started stealing and breaking into homes to obtain the money that we needed to buy drugs and alcohol. We no longer got together to play games. Instead, we gathered to smoke pot and drink cheap wine, or "bum juice" as we called it. I had become a street punk, believing that I was fighting the system. In reality, I was running away from my existence. To this day, there are many times when I still feel like this same "rebel without a cause."

As I look back upon my adolescence, I realize that I was very fortunate to have survived that stage of my pilgrimage. Unfortunately, many of my companions from those days self-destructed, succumbing to the many pressures that confronted us. I'm thankful that I recognized that, "I am not what society has taught me that I ought to be."[6] If I had simply accepted the identity dictated by my place in society, I would have given up my struggle. I would have remained a product of an environment dominated by an endless cycle of poverty, drugs, violence and crimes of all sort.

Reading psychotherapist Sheldon Kopp's popular book – *If You Meet the Buddha On the Road, Kill Him* – played a big role in justifying my desire to determine my own existence. However, if many of my peers had been reared in a more supportive and stable environment, instead of one that repeatedly emphasized failure and helplessness, they too may have developed the self-esteem needed to confront many of the struggles that they faced later in their lives.

So often, young people who are raised in these less-supportive environments are forced to grow up and assume adult responsibilities without having had the opportunity to enjoy their adolescence.

Kopp describes what so many children experience: "The most insidious of the premature responsibilities that may be foisted on some children is the expectation that the child is somehow supposed to take care of his parents, rather than the other way around." [7]

This was the case for me. Due to my father's alcoholism, my brothers and I were called upon to assume many adult responsibilities in an effort to help mom, who did not understand or speak English, and keep the family together. As pop went in and out of the hospital, I found myself in countless meetings with his doctor. I often translated very important information regarding my father's health between mom and the doctor.

My father suffered from complications associated with diabetes, including visual impairment and blood clots. His alcoholism and his failure to properly treat his diabetes led to further problems, causing him to be disabled by his late thirties. When pop wasn't in the hospital, he would be at home, drinking and waiting for my brothers and me to take care of him. Pop made himself out to be a victim, but as Kopp states, "The true victims were the other family members"[8]. I recall that pop no longer wanted to go upstairs to urinate and vomit; instead he had us place a bucket next to his bed so he could use it for those purposes. Every morning, someone was expected to empty it and place it back in its proper place before we left for school. God forgive us if this wasn't done on a timely basis, for pop would complain and frown that we did not care about him and were waiting for him to die.

Once again, Kopp accurately describes this situation. "It is my very strong impression that in such bargains, the victim is far more dangerous than the powerful, responsibility-burdened caretaker. Beware the helplessness gambit of the chronic victim! Some people typically get out from under their own responsibilities in difficult situations (in which they would otherwise have to take care of themselves) by acting helpless and weak in order to invite others to do for them. If the other person does not respond, then he is accused of being cruel and unfeeling. But should he arrogantly take on the role of caretaker, the helpless one will soon hold him in contempt as being a weak fool, and what he offers will be returned as somehow not good enough."[9]

Tension began to fill our home, as no one wanted to be pop's servant, and soon avoidance became the norm. My older brother was usually busy "escaping reality" with his friends and my younger brother was occupied with running numbers. Mom also began to give in to the burden, leaving me to become the caretaker for both of my parents. At the age of 15 – and without a driver's license – I was routinely driving mom to and from the hospital and doctor's appointments. During one meeting with pop's doctor, I was asked to translate for mom. The doctor asked us to consider placing pop in a nursing home because of health reasons. He also stressed that if we did not do so, and pop continued to drink, he would soon die. Upon translating this concern to mom, I noticed that she was looking at me for an answer. Mom would not assume the responsibility of making a decision regarding pop's destiny. There I was – a 15-year-old kid – having to make a decision that would determine the outcome of my 46-year-old father's life.

To this day, I believe that I made the right decision. Although pop continued to drink and only lived another four years, which was more than the doctor predicted, he was home with his family. My brothers and I sometimes debated whether I had made the right choice. Because of my decision, I often felt that they looked to me to assume total responsibility for pop. It was as though they were saying, "You had the opportunity to put him away and didn't, so you take care of him!"

The last four years of pop's life were very stressful for us all. Living with an alcoholic is an experience that no one should have to endure. What bothers me the most about the whole thing is that pop's bar mates always said what a good man he was. How I wished they could have been at our home when the door was locked at night.

Struggling College Years

Having survived the housing projects and life with an alcoholic father, I began to believe that my days of struggling were ending and that I would finally have a peaceful life. Instead, I soon became aware that "new solutions lead to new problems, new freedoms lead to new responsibilities."[10]

College represented the next challenge in the pilgrimage of my life. During my freshman year, new friends and experiences made things seem worthwhile. I accepted the educational challenge and did well that first year, despite having never been a good student and even being told once that I was not college material. Balancing my social life and studying never presented any major problems. I became happy with myself once again, enjoying being on my own, and being responsible only for myself. Looking back at my first year of college, I have only one regret: I should have enjoyed it more instead of feeling guilty for being happy. The good times would not last long.

My early college days were so happy that even circumstances that would have created a crisis for others seemed like minor nuisances to me. I was always broke. A few months earlier, my parents had chipped in to help me buy a car. I paid three hundred dollars for a 1973 Chevy Vega. But I was so strapped financially that I couldn't afford insurance. When the car failed to pass inspection, I couldn't afford to get it fixed or to replace it with another car. I continued driving with an expired inspection sticker and no insurance. Although I was stopped and cited by the police several times, I had to keep driving to get to school and to work.

Just keeping gas in the car was a challenge. One very cold night, I pulled into a full-service gas station with my gas gauge riding on empty. When the attendant came out, I gave her all the money I had, which totaled a whopping 53 cents. She wasn't happy, but it was all I had and I wanted to get home.

Sunday night was movie night on campus and when "Victor Victoria" was being shown, I wanted to see it because I'd heard it was funny. There was only one small problem: the admission price was 75 cents and I had no money. I spent the night walking around campus with nothing to do.

In addition to my financial hardships, there were also social issues to contend with. I shared a dorm room with Mike Hopkins, a black student from Philadelphia. Although there were only a few minority students in the dorm, everything seemed normal, and we had friendly relationships with the other undergrads that lived there. One night, after Mike and I returned from an evening class, we noticed that a letter had been slipped under our door. As I read it aloud, we were confronted by the racial hatred we both knew existed and had hoped to avoid.

We are watching you and we don't like what we see.
We don't want any n----- and sp---. Go home or else.
KKK.

Mike was outraged and ran into the hall, yelling for the cowards to come out. While I was just as angry, I doubted that anyone would come forward and assume responsibility for the letter. I also resolved that no threat would be enough to make me leave school. At the end of my freshman year, I drove home in my beat up Chevy Vega, knowing I would be back.

During that summer of 1983, I met my wife, Margarita. After having numerous meaningless relationships at college, I was looking for someone to settle down with. It was a happy time for both of us. Although we were just a couple of kids ourselves – I was 19 and she was 17 – we decided that we wanted a child. Soon after, I began to realize what a difficult road we would be traveling together.

Life's challenges continued to press me during the spring semester of my sophomore year. My father died in February and our son was born in April.

We rented an apartment, which meant that in addition to going to school full-time, I also worked two part-time jobs: one as an on-campus peer counselor and another as a night-shift security guard. Our apartment was actually a downgrade from the housing projects I had grown up in. Since we still couldn't make ends meet, we knew we would either have to resort to welfare or I would have to quit college. Since I knew I would regret leaving college, the choice seemed obvious to me.

I would leave home every morning before seven a.m., commute fifty miles, be in class by eight, spend time studying, and work my on-campus job before driving back home at about three p.m. At home, I would have dinner, watch the news and either study or spend time with my wife and son before leaving for work again. As a field supervisor for a security company, I drove from site to site, making sure that the guards were on duty. Finally, at one a.m., I could go home and get some rest, unless my son's crying awakened me during the night. I followed this schedule for the next two years.

If I'd wanted to give up, there was no shortage of excuses. While I knew that no one would blame me, somehow I sensed that I could endure and continued struggling along. By this time, I was two or three cars beyond my Chevy Vega, which had finally quit. But the other cars I could afford weren't much better. Many times, I had to push my car and pop the clutch just to get it started, and I never seemed to have enough money for gas. Since my wife didn't really understand that I was going to college to improve myself and provide a better life for our family, our relationship became tense. At times, Margarita asked me to quit college and get a real job. While I often considered this option, I knew that giving up wasn't the answer. I also recognized that we were just so young and life had become so difficult.

It would be selfish and egotistical to think that I kept going entirely on my own, without any support. There were two important people who helped me keep it together: Dr. Germain Francious, a professor in the Center for Educational Opportunities office, and Stuart Katzman, a professor in the criminal-justice department. These two men became my mentors, advisors and friends. They provided me with an overwhelming amount of support, encouragement and reassurance.

When our third child was born three years after my graduation, choosing his name – Germain Stuart Rosado – was easy. I could think of no better way to pay tribute to the two men who helped me reach a goal that seemed impossible a few years earlier, two men who taught me about responsibility and accountability, two men who taught me what it is to be a man.

While graduation was satisfying, it was only one of the tangible rewards I received for enduring those years of struggle. It took a few years for me to recognize the importance of an intangible reward I'd also earned, the knowledge that "whatever I gain will not change my life, and whatever pain I may have to endure, I will be able to survive."[11]

I am a survivor, one who continued to move forward despite the negative internal and external forces trying to conquer my will to succeed. While I can draw confidence from my past, I know that my biggest challenge confronts me today. Overcoming the challenge posed by this disease – the same one that killed my father and made living at home a nightmare – will require even greater courage and self-knowledge.

The time has come for me to deal with my own alcoholism. How could I allow this to happen after seeing what happened to pop and knowing what his drinking put us through? Asking "Why me?" is not going to provide any solutions; I must work through it. But there is hope for me because, unlike pop, I admit that I have a problem. I also firmly believe that "nothing about us can be changed until it is first accepted."[12] At times, it bothers me that I'm having so much trouble overcoming alcohol, despite having successfully stopped using marijuana and other drugs that I'd used for over ten years. Many times, I wonder whether or not I am losing my sanity, but I believe that the irresponsible act of "going crazy" – lashing out in a destructive, reckless and violent manner with no regard for myself or others – in order not to have to face up to the mess that I have created in my own life, is no solution for me. [13] Alcoholism has caused my life to become somewhat of a mess. Many people may be surprised to know that Mr. Rosado, a college graduate and high school guidance counselor, goes home at the end of the workday and is transformed into JoJo the alcoholic.

Looking back at how alcohol affected my life, from pop's alcoholism to my own, I dread to think what will become of my family and me if I do not overcome this disease. I understand that no man can recover his own beauty and innocence without first facing the ugliness and evil in himself.[14] Therefore, "I must be ready to confront feelings and ideas within myself that are ugly, evil and discrediting, if I am to receive the lovely, tender, decent aspects of myself."[15] The presence of alcohol in my life has made my pilgrimage a living hell at times, but I refuse to allow it, or anything else, to alter my destiny.

I move forward in my journey with a firmer understanding of my struggle for salvation. While my life has been difficult, I gain inspiration from the thought that no matter how bad off I am, others have overcome much more. I continue on this pilgrimage knowing that at times I will become upset with myself and feel depressed and lonely. "It is true that I must continue to struggle but how strange, that so often, it all seems worth it."[16]

I'm grateful for the opportunity to look back over my pilgrimage and re-assess my life in a new light. I'm comforted with the knowledge that "the openness to salvation must be re-asserted again and again and again. The only way to be saved is to spend your lifetime on a pilgrimage."[17]

Crossing Over

June 20, 1986 is the day that I "crossed over." For the first 18 years of my life, I was classified as a poor, at-risk teen who was delinquent, truant and not college material, among other things. Four years later, upon graduating from college, I was an "exception to the rule." The rule being that poor, inner-city, minority kids raised on welfare don't graduate from college.

One month after my graduation, I was asked to speak at the Bethlehem Area School District's (BASD) minority student awards ceremony. Although the other speaker was a prominent doctor, the attention I received at the end of the ceremonies was overwhelming. Even Dr. Willis was impressed with my story. The following school year, I was hired by the BASD as a guidance counselor. Ever since, I've been asked the same question hundreds of times. People always inquire, "What made the difference for you?" It's as though I possess the secret for overcoming the barriers that confront today's youth.

As I noted earlier, after joining the professional ranks, I continued to live on both sides of the tracks for several years. Continuing to engage in these self-limiting and self-destructive behaviors presented obvious problems in my professional life. Crossing back and forth from the streets of the projects into the professional world was like trying to walk a tightrope in a windstorm. Sooner or later, I was going to fall and fall hard. Not only was I on the verge of destroying my professional career, more importantly, I was on the verge of destroying my family too.

Changes had to be made; the cycle had to be broken. For the first two years of my career as a high school counselor, I continued to live in the housing projects and engaged in the public consumption of alcohol. I was not a role model; I was a hypocrite. I preached one thing to my students during the day and contradicted myself at night.

For me, the first step was moving out of the projects. As a teenager, I often dreamed about owning my own house and raising my family in a better environment. The physical move was the easy part of the journey. Becoming sober proved to be more difficult; even two alcohol-related arrests had no effect on me. The first arrest occurred while I was still in college. I was arrested for disorderly conduct after a fight broke out during a house party in the projects, a fight that included weapons and numerous injuries. My second arrest was for driving under the influence (DUI). Even though I lost my driving privileges for two and half years as a result of my DUI arrest, and relied on my wife to drive me to and from work, I continued to drink.

The longer I walked this tightrope, the stronger the windstorm grew. I knew I could not avoid the big fall much longer. Fortunately for me, the student sometimes has insights to share with the teacher. On May 3, 1990, a comment from one of my students convinced me that the time had come for me to stop drinking. Simply put, it's the most difficult thing I have ever done.

I was once guilty of Being Good at Being Bad; I was part of the problem. Now I believe that I've become part of the solution. I once told a newspaper reporter that if I had to relive my life over one hundred times, I would not be so fortunate as to end up where I am now. Jail or death would claim me at least ninety times – I truly believe this.

Both my personal and professional experiences have compelled me to write this book. Although I do not claim to have all the answers, I believe I can offer a unique, realistic perspective on many of the issues confronting today's youth, along with strategies and proposals to bring about a real difference.

Prepare to go beyond the status quo and question the social issues, the political barriers and the hypocrisy that keep ALL of our youth at risk.

Disclaimer

The Root of Evil

Any perspective on the causes of social deviance and the factors that contribute to violence and aggression among our youth must address the question, "Are some kids born to be bad?" The nature-versus-nurture argument remains the topic of much debate among behavioral scientists. Although this debate must be acknowledged, my position was made clear in Section I: Nurture Rules

However, I will concede that I believe a very small percentage of people are going to be bad regardless of the nurturing – good or bad – they experience. Unlike people who suffer from medical conditions – such as depression, anxiety disorders, or schizophrenia – these sociopaths are seemingly healthy people who feel free to go out and commit crimes with no regard for the feelings or property of others. After interviewing dozens of teenage killers, Shawn Johnson, a forensic psychologist in Sacramento, CA, concluded, "I guess the bottom line for me is that evil exists."[1]

Thankfully, sociopaths are rare freaks of nature. When behavioral experts view an act or a series of acts as evil, they may classify the offender as a sociopath. They may argue that "by all accounts," the individual came from a good home, was a good student and appeared to be a well-adjusted and responsible person. The flaw in this thinking is that we can never totally account for the individual's life experiences, the impact those experiences had on the individual, and to what extent those experiences contributed to the criminal act.

The nature-versus-nurture argument was put to the test after the Columbine shootings. The lives of shooters Eric Harris and Dylan Klebold, who were responsible for killing 12 students and a teacher, continue to be dissected and analyzed. Behavioral experts are still trying to understand what led these two high-school teenagers to plan and carry out their homicidal rage before taking their own lives on April 20, 1999.

More recently, on April 16, 2007, Cho Seung- Hui carried out the Virginia Tech Massacre, the worst shooting in United States history. Although the warning signs Cho displayed may have been an indicator of what he was capable of, apparently it wasn't enough to confine or commit him prior to his onslaught. The warning signs he displayed and the "manifesto" he provided will certainly continue to fuel the nature-versus-nurture debate.

There are three areas that contribute a great deal toward the development of every individual and account for the vast majority of life experiences during childhood and adolescence. These areas are the individual's home, community and schools. The nurturing that each person receives in these areas mold and shape their character. This concept closely parallels the notion that, "It takes a village to raise a child." In the end, it's the nurturing that children receive in their home, their community and their schools – both good and bad – that may determine that person's perspective on life, thus having an influence on the individual's behaviors.

Assistant U.S. Attorney Kathy Stark reinforced this position during a gang prevention summit. As she presented several investigations conducted by her office on drug gangs, she detailed shootings and violent homicides committed by the subjects of the federal investigations. She went on to say, "These individuals have no redeemable qualities...they are not redeemable." Whether you agree with this assertion or not, we must contend with the factors which led the individuals to engage in such violent acts. Are these gang bangers, and the thousands like them across the country, natural born criminals – destined to be homicidal – or are they products of their environment? Without making excuses, I believe their life experiences are significant contributing factors.

Beginning in the next section, I will demonstrate how a "strike" in any one of these three areas can contribute to an individual's involvement in crime, violence or other forms of antisocial behavior.

For me, the bottom line is clear – Good nurturing can make up for many of nature's mistakes; a lack of nurturing or poor nurturing can trash nature's best efforts. Nurture rules.[2]

Section II

Strike 1: Failure on the Home Front

Jimmy is Angry; He is Also "In Charge"

While serving as a counselor at Liberty High School, I interacted primarily with young people from low-income, drug-infested, and crime-riddled neighborhoods. Many of my students were raised in dysfunctional homes and subjected to verbal, emotional and/or physical abuse. Having grown up under similar circumstances, I was in my element dealing with these life and death issues on a regular basis. The kids I worked with were confronting teen pregnancies, drug abuse, suicidal thoughts, suicide attempts, and everything in between.

Moving to East Hills – with its middle- to upper-middle-class clientele – was supposed to be a different world. It was. During my first week, I dealt with one student suffering from school phobia and a sixth-grade girl who was devastated because the friends she'd had since kindergarten were growing apart. After eight years of life-and-death situations, these issues seemed trivial. I quickly realized that no matter how insignificant an individual's crisis may seem to others or how they compare to other life stressors, it's nonetheless a crisis for that person at that time.

East Hills also helped me see that middle-class suburbia isn't synonymous with a Brady Bunch existence. About two months into the school year, I met with Jimmy, a student who was not doing well academically and who was exhibiting aggressive, disruptive and defiant behaviors at school. After several meetings with Jimmy and numerous conferences with his team of teachers, I decided to have a meeting with his parents.

While I'd interacted with middle-class students before, I'd only had limited interactions with students and parents together. Because Jimmy's parents were divorced and shared custody, his mom and stepfather attended the first meeting. What occurred during that session said it all. When Jimmy's mother offered her thoughts, Jimmy said, "What do you know; you're stupid." When his stepfather dared to offer his perspective, Jimmy responded, "Shut the f--- up; you're not my father." It was obvious that we had a lot of work to do. A few weeks later, we again called for another parental meeting. While this meeting involved different participants – his dad and stepmom – the results were similar. During each meeting, I made it clear to Jimmy that his behavior toward his parents was unacceptable to me, especially in my office. Trying to impose my values on Jimmy was not the answer.

Despite all of my parents' mistakes, one thing they instilled in me was respect for family, respect for adults, and respect for authority. It became apparent that Jimmy was being raised in a dysfunctional home and that his parents' divorce made Jimmy angry. It was also becoming obvious that Jimmy, at the age of 12, had assumed control of his parents. He did this by making them feel guilty. Their attempts to make up for their shortcomings as parents, together with their failures to provide him with a well-structured family, were simply enabling Jimmy. Because they were *parenting with guilt,* they were reinforcing his negative behaviors.

As I saw more and more families and witnessed the effects of parenting with guilt, I realized that middle-class America is as dysfunctional as any other segment of society. I'll expand further on parenting with guilt in the next chapter. As for Jimmy, a newspaper reported several years later that he had been arrested for robbery. I also heard that he became involved with drugs. Sadly, I was not surprised.

Home Sweet Home It's Not – Strike One

The deterioration of the family structure is frequently identified as a leading cause for the escalating rise of youth violence in America. Countless studies and reports provide statistics that detail the factors associated with dysfunctional homes.

Prior to looking at any such statistics, we should further explore the concept of *parenting with guilt* (PWG). As noted earlier, PWG is present when parents are influenced by a guilt complex connected to their failure to provide for the needs of their children. Factors that lead to PWG include, but are not limited to:

- Absent Parent(s) – Placing personal or professional interests before the needs of the children and family (personal interests include social and recreational activities; professional interests are job or career related.)
- Abusive Parent(s) – When a parent inflicts verbal, emotional and/or physical abuse upon their children or toward one another.
- Poverty/Financial Hardships – The lack of financial stability.
- Parental Substance Abuse – Drug or alcohol abuse by parents.
- Broken Home – Parental separation, divorce and stepfamilies.

All of these circumstances are connected to some real or imagined feelings of failure in the parent, feelings that cause them to act from a sense of guilt. While the parent experiences guilt and failure, children who internalize the same parental shortcomings become angry.

Armed with this anger, children may display a variety of deviant, anti-social, delinquent, or other self-limiting behaviors. These behaviors might extend to criminal or violent acts, drug and alcohol abuse, self-mutilation, or school failure. Children may also lash out at parents or fail to respond to a parent's repeated attempts to "parent" them during adolescence. For example, an absent parent who fails to provide sufficient structure and discipline during childhood creates a void in the relationship that will be tested during adolescence. When an adolescent becomes involved in self-limiting behaviors, he or she is resisting any attempts by a parent to intervene or assume control. The adolescent is manipulating the guilty parent with these refusals to comply. Because of these guilty feelings, the parent fails to assume control and set appropriate boundaries, which enables the adolescent to retain control.

Later, we will explore how PWG restricts a parent's ability to intervene appropriately regarding concerns about their children in our communities and in our schools. For now, we have established that a dysfunctional home is one that has PWG in operation.

That PWG environment and the associated failure of the family structure are the equivalent of a setback that we'll call *strike one*.

Assessing the Guilt/Anger Factor by the Numbers:
The Absent Parent(s)

- In 69% of all married couples having children between six and 17 years old, both parents work outside of the home[1].

- In 71% of single-mother families and 85% of single-father families with children aged six to 17, the custodial parent works outside of the home[2].

- More than 70% of employed parents who spend more than 40 hours per week on the job feel that they do not have enough time with their children[3].

These figures only account for a parent's absence due to employment factors. You can predict the potential void in the family by considering the amount of time parents may spend in social and recreational activities without their children.

At some point, this void may emphasize failure. This sense of failure leads to a counterproductive relationship between a guilty parent and an angry child.

Establishing a Healthy, Productive Balance

Life consists of numerous relationships. How we manage or balance these relationships determine whether a relationship is healthy or unhealthy, productive or counter-productive. In order to establish a healthy, productive relationship with their children, parents must assess their time investments in their job, family time, and recreational interests.

Certain time constraints are non-negotiable. For example, job or career responsibilities can place heavy demands on a parent's time. Certainly, providing for a family's financial needs is a priority. However, when faced with the opportunity of pursuing career aspirations that demand increasing time away, parents must assess how those demands will affect their relationship with their children. Placing career aspirations before the needs of their children could create an unhealthy, counterproductive void in the family. At times, it may be in the family's best interest for parents to place more demanding career aspirations "on hold." This is especially important while the children are young.

Establishing a solid parent-child relationship requires an investment of quality time. Quality time means providing structure and discipline, establishing trust and communication, and becoming comfortable with each other.

In addition to assessing job and career responsibilities, parents must also balance their social and recreational activities with the well being of their children. The responsibility of being a parent, of being part of a family unit, must supercede any social or recreational interests. This commitment begins at birth and continues throughout adolescence.

Parents must be cautious that they don't fall into the trap of thinking "I will be there when my child needs me." By this time, it may be too late and the void may have already strained the relationship. It's not sufficient to begin parenting a child during adolescence.

Assessing the Guilt/Anger Factor by the Numbers:
The Abusive Parent(s)

- In 1999, Child Protective Services (CPS) agencies handled an estimated 3 million cases of alleged child abuse.[4]

- Child maltreatment reports have grown steadily over the past 10 years, with the total number of reports nationwide increasing 45% since 1987.[5]

- Nationally, of the children for whom allegations of abuse were proven:

  - 56% were neglected
  - 25% were physically abused
  - 13% were sexually abused
  - 6% were emotionally abused
  - 13% were classified as suffering from some other form of maltreatment.[6]

- A child's exposure to the father's abuse of the mother is the greatest risk factor for bridging violent behavior from one generation to the next.[7]

Given these factors, it is understandable that living in an abusive home may emphasize failure. This failure may be internalized as either guilt in the parents or as anger in the children.

Halting the Abuse

As indicated by my brief autobiography, it is very difficult to assess what really goes on behind closed doors in any given household. Because of this, countless cases of abuse will go undetected. Given this, it is imperative that those cases that are reported be fully investigated and allotted the appropriate resources to protect the victims. Unfortunately, most resources designated for child protection are invested in the screening, investigation and substantiation of the millions of abuse reports received by states each year. This practice leaves few resources for services to troubled families. This means that the Child Protective Services (CPS) system is not addressing most of the fundamental factors associated with child maltreatment – which include poverty, substance abuse and social isolation.

Regardless of the severity of the alleged abuse, most states respond to reports of child abuse with a remarkably standardized investigation.[8] The United States spends more money annually to battle child abuse than any other country in the world, yet each year more children suffer.[9]

Reforming our CPS systems is imperative. In fact, many states have begun this critical process and have identified the important factors. The most recent initiatives in comprehensive CPS reform consist of several key components:

- **Planning for legislative change.** Planning for CPS reform involves determining the views and concerns of a wide array of stakeholders, including families and CPS workers, as well as identifying community values.

- **Use of family-centered assessments.** Having legislative authorization for flexibility in responding to reports of abuse and neglect is central to CPS reform. Serious criminal offenses against children should be subject to investigation and prosecution. However, CPS should be able to respond with an assessment of family strengths and appropriate services to less serious allegations.

- **Changes to central abuse registry.** Registries are controversial because they often label caretakers as abusers, regardless of the severity of the maltreatment or the circumstances. In keeping with the new role of CPS as a family-serving agency, legislatures in some states are limiting the use of central registries.

- **Clarification of the role of law-enforcement agencies in the investigation of child abuse.** In many cases, CPS reform legislation addresses a lack of coordination between police and CPS agencies investigating criminal child abuse. Some states are referring child-protective investigations to law-enforcement agencies, freeing CPS agencies from the role conflict that's inherent in being both investigator and helper.

- **Collaboration between CPS agencies and communities.** Legislatures in a few states are calling for partnerships between CPS agencies and neighborhood-based systems of family support, such as schools, churches, community organizations and mental health providers. The premise underlying these initiatives is that the responsibility for child protection should be shared by the various individuals and organizations that are in contact with children and families.

- **Implementation strategies.** Some states are experimenting with CPS reform through pilot programs, while others have enacted immediate statewide change. The choice between these two implementation strategies depends upon the political environment, the capacity of the CPS system, and other factors.

- **Outcome evaluation.** Legislators need information about the results of experiments in CPS reform to make intelligent decisions about expanding, continuing or terminating new programs. As a result, most state legislatures that have enacted CPS reform have included an evaluation component.[10]

State legislatures play a vital role in the CPS reform process. They define child abuse, mandate who must report child abuse, structure and designate funds for child welfare agencies, and prescribe CPS functions. State law regarding CPS is influenced by federal funding statues that prescribe standards for identifying, reporting and responding to child abuse.[11] Given this, the potential for effective and meaningful reform is within reach. The only question to ask is: What priority will our state and federal governments place on protecting our children from abuse?

The momentum to reform our CPS system has heightened due to the negative media attention revolving around several high-profile cases across the country. These cases include children in foster-care placement in Florida and other states that are unaccounted for, as well as the death of a New Jersey child under the protection of "the system," an occurrence that went undetected for months. The biggest challenge now is for our state and federal bureaucrats to overcome the political obstacles and political hypocrisies that perpetuate the status quo.

The truth is that the protection of our children has never been a political priority. Regardless of what statistics may indicate from year to year, those who work most closely with our children – social workers, educators, law-enforcement agencies, and others – admit that children in America are not safe.

Those who threaten our children come from various fronts. Some are strangers lurking in the shadows or on the Internet. Some are within a child's circles of trust – teachers, coaches, day-care workers, religious personnel and youth advocates. As always, the greatest danger to children comes from within their own families. Child abuse continues to be a horrific reality within our society. In spite of this, addressing it is never on the national agenda.[12]

To conclude the points made in this chapter, I offer a letter I sent to the editor of *The Express-Times* newspaper in October 1993. Although I wrote this letter over a decade ago, it is just as relevant and to the point now as it was then.

Originally published in *The Express-Times* (Easton, PA), December 9, 1993

Appropriate alternatives and resources will do more to reduce youth crime than legislation

Recently our state representatives introduced bills intended to make gun owners more responsible in securing their weapons and penalizing those that fail to do so if their weapons are used to commit a crime.

The state House of Representatives also unanimously approved a bill overhauling our child protective laws.

As a parent, coach and educator, I agree that these issues must be addressed, but I don't believe that new legislation, on its own, will provide the solutions we seek.

As a counselor in the Bethlehem Area School District, I unfortunately come into contact with many young victims of abuse.

This, in itself, is very bothersome, but it does not compare to the frustration we confront when we realize how limited our resources are in regard to children and youth services and emergency services.

Many times, it appears that the helping agencies are overwhelmed with referrals. It has also been my experience that abused teenagers often find themselves on our streets as runaways, and are not considered priorities due to the many cases involving younger children.

In one of my classes, a student stated that the newest trend calls for teenagers to carry guns primarily to gain status among their peers.

When our children turn toward carrying guns as a fashion statement or to be recognized as tough, no legislation can serve as a deterrent. In fact, most students I spoke with were unaware that the legislation regarding firearms was introduced, and said that the threat of incarceration does not serve as a deterrent.

It is quite apparent that our adolescent population seeks positive alternatives to the streets and protection from abuse inflicted by parents and others.

Our elected officials can provide the resources that will be needed to implement the appropriate alternatives. They can redirect/reprioritize where and how our tax dollars are used.

It makes no sense when an abused child cannot receive the help that he/she requires because of limited resources. Yet, when that individual eventually acts out and gets involved in delinquent/criminal behavior, we can accommodate him or her in our detention centers and jails at a much higher cost.

As long as we continue to pass legislation designed to regulate behavior without providing positive alternatives to those behaviors, the problems will continue.

As long as we make building jails/prisons our priority, we will always keep them full while the crime and abuse continues.

Assessing the Guilt/Anger Factor by the Numbers:
Poverty/Financial Hardships

Poverty and financial hardship have a significant relationship to the maltreatment of children, according to the third National Incidence Study (NIS-3) of child maltreatment, released by the National Center on Child Abuse and Neglect (NCCAN). Children whose family income fell below the poverty level were:

- 22 times more likely to experience maltreatment
- 44 times more likely to be neglected
- 22 times more likely to be seriously injured
- 60 times more likely to die from maltreatment

These figures clearly demonstrate that children living in conditions of poverty and financial hardship face a greater risk of abuse. Children living in hardship often become angry and conclude that life is not fair. Their anger may be directed at "the system," and they may believe the system discriminates against them and their parents. Adolescents armed with this anger may adopt anti-social or anti-establishment behaviors, which may include delinquent or illegal acts.

These children are also more likely to become angry with their parent(s), especially if they have been abused. Anger directed at a parent can also stem from the adolescent's resentment toward a parent. This resentment could be fueled by the adolescent's perception of a parent as weak, unable, or unwilling to overcome their financial situation.

Making the Most of a Little

Living in poverty or experiencing prolonged financial hardship is not a crime, nor should it be viewed as a social plague. There are many factors that contribute to an individual's financial situation, including the individual's education, job or career training, employment opportunities, the current economic climate, and the individual's domestic situation.

Although there are no simple solutions, the individual's resiliency and the resiliency of the family may be the determining factors regarding how well the individual and the family cope with the situation. Those families who are most resilient may seek assistance from government entitlement programs for the poor, and find solace in their unity and the support of family and friends. With pride and determination, poverty and prolonged financial hardships can be overcome and the cycle of failure can be broken. Those families that seek assistance in time of need, in an effort to become self-sufficient, are more likely to escape the cycle of dependency and failure.

However, for those families with additional stressors such as the maltreatment of children and parental substance abuse, the problems are compounded. These families are more likely to become dependent on government entitlement programs for the poor, engage in fraud, and only fall deeper into despair.

Bastardizing Our Children

It was a hot summer day. I was six or seven years old. Mom called me into the house and asked me to go to the housing office to pay the rent. As she handed me the money and rent statement, she said, "If they ask you if your father lives here, say no." I looked at her and said, "But he does live here." It was true that while he was not home much, his clothes were upstairs and he slept in the house. Still, mom made it clear that if I were asked, I was to say no. So I was off to pay the rent.

Walking and running to the office, I forgot what mom had just told me. I just wanted to hurry so that I could go back to playing with my friends. As I entered the office and approached the counter, I became nervous. I remembered what mom told me. At the counter, I looked up at the office clerk behind the glass and passed the rent money and statement through to her. She took it, stamped the statement and gave it back to me as a receipt – no questions asked.

After this, I was back to playing with my friends and enjoying being a kid. But this would not be the last time that mom would ask me to lie about pop. A few years later, I realized why mom asked me to do what she did. If pop had been on our lease, our rent would have been higher and our welfare benefits would have been much lower. Even though pop often gave us a reprieve by moving out or going to Puerto Rico for weeks at a time, he always returned to live with us. The truth is that most people in the projects were living that way – they still are. How can I be certain of this? I still see it happening. I've seen it in both my personal and professional relationships.

As a school administrator, I see applications for free and reduced lunch that list only one adult and one household income. Many times, I see forms that indicate a single parent or female head-of-household. In many cases, I'm aware that another adult, typically a father or stepfather, is part of the family. Is this cheating? Obviously. The question is: Who's really being cheated? When children are told to lie about their parents' domestic arrangements so that the family can pay less to live in the projects, qualify for food stamps, receive free health care, free school lunches and other government entitlements for the poor, we have created a cycle grounded in deceit and failure. Many individuals living like this may feel justified in cheating the system. They may believe the system owes them something. Others just see it as easy money for enhancing or enabling a lifestyle. In our household, pop's disability income, the money my younger brother was pulling in running numbers for pop, and our welfare benefits should have afforded us the ability to live above the poverty level. However, as is often the case in similar households, most of pop's income and the numbers money was reserved for pop's vices – drinking and gambling. Therefore, poverty was our reality.

More than 20 years later, my mother continues to pay the price. Living out of wedlock – for the sake of qualifying for welfare benefits – disqualified her from receiving my father's pension upon his death. This loss far exceeds any amount of welfare checks.

In addition to cheating the welfare program, individuals and families seeking to defraud the system for financial gain may become familiar with other government entitlement programs that they can scam. The Supplemental Security Income (SSI) program is one of these. Administered by the Social Security Administration, SSI provides supplemental income for disabled individuals. Many adults fake mental illnesses or health problems in an attempt to qualify for an SSI check. What's worse is that many parents, especially neglectful and abusive parents, coach their children to fake these ailments so they can become eligible. The actual cash benefits that the child may be eligible for depends on the family income. By not reporting the father or another male provider on the application, they're reporting a lower household income, thus maximizing the cash benefits for an eligible child.

Eventually, most families practicing this type of deceit perpetuate this lifestyle for themselves and for their children. This cycle of failure contributes to the breakdown of the family unit and promotes parents living out of wedlock. It keeps families in government-subsidized housing and discourages home ownership. And it leads to generation after generation of bastardized children – children who lack good work ethics, children who look for shortcuts and instant gratification instead of setting their own long-term goals. It creates children who may not be willing to pursue higher education, including college, because they are not willing to invest the time it takes to earn a degree. In addition to fostering a cycle that's ripe with fraud and deceit, it breeds a pattern of dependency and failure in the next generation.

These programs – welfare, SSI and others – are intended to provide assistance, not a lifestyle or a form of dependency. The fraud associated with these entitlement programs costs taxpayers millions of dollars each year. However, the cost paid by children raised with this deceit can be much higher, as they may never reach their full potential as individuals or as parents of the next generation of bastards. The cycle is difficult to break. Change, on a larger scale, will only be possible if we replace entitlement programs that promote fraud and dependency with programs that promote family and education.

This is especially vital for those families that are truly in need of public assistance. Providing assistance must include a realistic goal of making the family self-sufficient. Viable employment opportunities that provide a decent living wage, along with accessible and affordable health care, must factor into the equation.

As for the cost to taxpayers, the fraud associated with entitlement programs for the poor does not come close to the cost of the fraud and abuse committed by other segments of our society. Tax fraud, tax evasion and "corporate welfare" cost taxpayers hundreds of billions of dollars, dwarfing any fraud associated with welfare and other programs for the poor. In addition to corporate welfare, corporate America also benefits from the fraud and dependency associated with entitlement programs for the poor. A generation of children – including an over-represented number from poor and low-income households – is being over-identified with behavioral, social, emotional and psychological disabilities and prescribed various "meds." In the process, pharmaceutical companies are taking in billions of dollars each year. For the pharmaceutical companies, the labels that are put on these kids – such as attention-deficit disorder (ADD), attention-deficit hyperactivity disorder (ADHD), central auditory processing disorder (CAPD) and obsessive-compulsive disorder (OCD) – along with a host of other disorders, translates into big profits.

There appears to be little concern that giving these meds to children and adolescents may contribute to later drug or alcohol abuse. Prescription drugs such as Ritalin, Xanax and others often find their way onto the streets to become part of the drug market. This flood of prescription drugs contributes further to the bastardization of our children and increases the number put in foster care and those orphaned by the unregulated drug market.

Assessing the Guilt/Anger Factor by the Numbers:
Parental Substance Abuse

- Parental substance abuse is a factor in more than 75% of cases in New York City where children are placed in foster care.[13]

- Children raised in homes with parental substance abuse are at risk for poor academic outcomes, receive less parental supervision and encouragement, are more likely to be absent from school, lack clean clothes and miss meals.[14]

The hardship associated with growing up in a household where a parent or other adult caregiver abuses alcohol or other drugs was portrayed in the first section of this book. The supporting data provided above should not be required to establish that parental substance abuse has a negative impact on children and emphasizes failure. Anyone raised in a home where at least one parent engaged in substance abuse with drugs or alcohol understands how devastating it can be.

Unfortunately, many children of alcoholics and addicts repeat the mistakes of their parents. Any police officer who has responded to a "domestic" call where substance abuse was evident and children were present can predict future trauma and hardship. Social services personnel and school officials – including teachers, counselors and administrators – have also seen the signs, both subtle and blatant.

The harm is being done. The only question is, can it be halted? The answer will not be found in either statistics or personal anecdotes.

Sobriety Required

Sobriety saves lives. Sobriety saves families. However, as I noted in my own story, sobriety may be the most difficult goal for someone to accomplish. Despite that, it must be the first step in any efforts to reconcile relationships and minimize damage. These matters are further complicated by the guilt/anger factor, which stresses the relationship between parents and their children.

A commitment to sobriety, a commitment to family, a commitment to raise your children in a healthy environment, can be successful. The guilt/anger factor can be overcome. As they say, it is easier said than done. Understand this, "The truth shall set you free, but first it will make you miserable." Reestablishing trust and communication is vital. Professional help, in the form of a counselor or therapist, can help the process. Counseling can also help children understand addiction as a disease, which may help them to avoid using alcohol and other drugs.

If the person with the alcohol or drug problem won't pursue sobriety, the only viable options are to remove the abuser or the children from the home. In most cases, the unfortunate likelihood is that none of the above will occur.

Assessing the Guilt/Anger Factor by the Numbers:
Broken Homes

- A study of 25,000 incarcerated juveniles conducted by the Bureau of Justice Statistics indicated that 72% came from broken homes.[15]
- A child raised in a single parent home (usually female-headed) is seven times as likely to be a delinquent. [16]
- Children of stepfamily households have the same frequency of problems as children in single-parent families. [17]
- Children and divorce:
    - 31% report they are fine
    - 33% report they are somewhat angry
    - 19% report they are quite angry
    - 17% report they are extremely angry[18]

The inability of parents to maintain an intact, well-structured household can be the most significant circumstance contributing to the guilt/anger factor. The bond between a parent and a child should be the strongest bond a child has, at least throughout childhood and into adolescence. When the bond between a child and a parent is severed during this crucial time, it promotes guilt and anger.

As the numbers indicate, 69% of children of divorce report a sense of anger. This anger significantly increases a child's likelihood of becoming involved in delinquent behavior. Anger can also be a factor contributing to the difficulties experienced by stepfamilies, which can include children of divorce. Children of divorce may also use their anger to manipulate the guilt of parents.

For the Children's Sake

Separation and divorce have become national epidemics. Although most couples who separate or divorce justify the split by citing financial problems, infidelity, stress, substance abuse, other forms of abuse or irreconcilable differences, many couples that don't split overcome these same hardships. Many times, the only difference is adhering to a commitment to family, which may include seeking counseling, establishing honest and open communication, reassessing priorities, and having the resolve to fulfill the responsibilities of being a spouse and a parent.

Overcoming the hardships that couples face is hard work. Couples without children may not be as committed to investing the time and energy that is required to overcome certain hardships. Couples with children may find that this bond provides an incentive to commit to the work required to keep the family intact.

Sometimes, it becomes apparent that the circumstances generating the hardship are not likely to change, even after attempts to resolve or remedy the problem. In cases where the dysfunctional or culpable parent is contributing to the demise of the family, it may be best that they not remain part of the household.

Simply put, some families are better off as single-parent households. A single-parent household is a better environment than a two-parent household where one parent is engaged in substance abuse or is inflicting abuse on others.

Party Parents!

Growing up, it was common knowledge that parents "partied," often in excess. We knew which ones were the drinkers, the pill poppers and the junkies. Not to be outdone, abusing drugs and alcohol as teenagers was a way of life for my peers and me. More often than not, we had little or no trouble getting our hands on whatever we wanted. Most drugs, including prescription drugs, were readily available and alcohol was in abundance. When money was tight, someone within the group was able to tap into their parents' supply – usually of alcohol and prescription drugs. Tapping into a parent's stash was acceptable to us because they always had access to more booze and more pills. However, the idea of partying with our parents, or with their consent, was unthinkable for most of us. Aside from being illegal, we saw it as immoral.

Even though we were getting high – often off a parent's supply – there was still a level of respect that existed for most of us, a line that could not be crossed. In a strange way, it's similar to the code of honor among thieves. We knew that our parents would not be in favor of our drug and alcohol use, and that they would certainly not give our partying their consent or look the other way.

There were a limited few for whom the experience of getting high with their parents – or with their consent – was normal. I recall a few guys that I met in junior and senior high sharing how they partied with their parents. Of course, they referred to these parents as "cool." Some came from middle-class backgrounds, while at least two came from broken homes, where their parents were divorced. One of them, Scott, often shared how he and his mom got high together, and how it brought them closer together. He considered her his friend. Some of the guys that partied with them also thought it was cool. We were 14 and 15 years old.

As a teen, partying with my parents was out of the question. As a parent, partying with my own children, their friends or their peer group would be the ultimate betrayal. Unfortunately, many adults do not share my sentiment on this issue. For whatever reason – guilt, the need for acceptance, wanting to appear cool or just plain stupidity – they condone and even participate in the drug and alcohol use of their children and their child's peer groups. One report from the National Center on Addiction and Substance Abuse at Columbia University reported that some parents encourage substance abuse with their own conduct. They found that 25 percent of teenagers between the ages of 15 and 17 have attended a party in the past two years at which parents purchased or served alcohol to underage teens.[19] These people must be held accountable – and now they are.

April 29, 2001 was a day of tragedy that led to a precedent-setting verdict in Northampton County, PA. On this day, two 18 year olds and one 19 year old left a drinking party attended by close to 50 other teenagers. The trio was killed when the sport utility vehicle driven by the 19 year old – who had a blood/alcohol ratio of 0.20 – crashed.

The woman who hosted the underage drinking party, along with her teenage daughter, were charged and convicted of involuntary manslaughter. Judith McCloskey's conviction was the first of its type not only in Pennsylvania, but also in the United States.

Northampton County District Attorney John Morganelli said in a statement following the verdict, "Any and all adults in Pennsylvania are now on notice that they can be prosecuted criminally on charges of involuntary manslaughter if they intentionally give alcohol to minors which results in the death of the minors related to the alcohol."

Judith McCloskey served the minimum sentence of one year in prison. The State Superior Court upheld her conviction.

José – 1980 Pennsylvania Golden Gloves,
Northeast District, Welterweight Champion (147 lbs.).

José celebrates the opening of the Bethlehem Boxing club
with Angel Marrero.

Neighborhood heroin addict laid out on a front porch.
(Photo by José Rosado)

Children play on a discarded sofa and mattresses in a park
littered with broken bottles and used "needles."
(Photo by José Rosado)

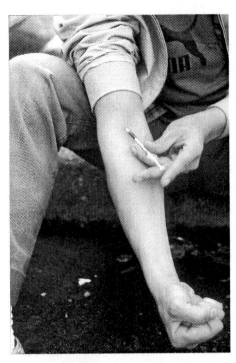

Teen heroin addict "shoots up" while sitting in a parking lot.
(Photo by José Rosado)

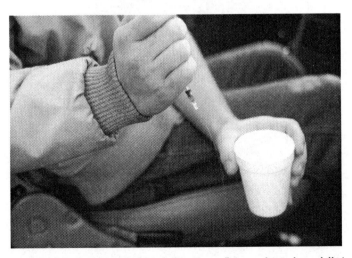

After using a "needle" to "shoot up," teen heroin addict
rinses the "needle" with water before he passes it on to the
next person for his use. (Photo by José Rosado)

Students facilitate the Listen Up Talk Show Program at
Liberty High School (Bethlehem, PA.).
(Photo provided by The Morning Call)

José embraces Angel Torres, the recipient of the first David
Sanchez Memorial Award, at Broughal Middle School
(Bethlehem, PA.) during the Homecoming Assembly.
(Photo provided by The Morning Call)

Section III

Strike 2: Failure in the Community

Fighting Mad

What festers in the home does not necessarily stay in the home. The anger that consumed me throughout my adolescence and early teen years found an outlet – fighting. Although, I had been fighting since elementary school, the fighting became much more frequent and more violent in junior high school and high school. As I mentioned earlier, no real reason was ever needed. I was not a bully; I fought others that were just as angry and eager to fight as I was. I fought those who would bully others; I fought friends and unknowns. I fought straight up – with no weapons. If my opponent brought a weapon into the fight – usually a baseball bat, pipe, bottle, nunchucks or other objects –I would grab whatever I could.

Recalling this stage of my life, I recognize how fortunate I was that guns were not readily available or commonly used in street fights. By today's standards and expectations, I most certainly would have been involved in fights involving guns.

One fight led to a life-altering and maybe a life-saving encounter. During a summer festival known as The Christmas City Festival, I was at it again. I was high, angry and looking for conflict. A short time after arriving at the festival, I found someone to accommodate me, or maybe I was accommodating him. The fight erupted suddenly, and just as suddenly the crowed encircled us. As the punches flew, I knocked my opponent to the ground. As I moved forward to pounce on him, I was jerked back and pulled away. The person who removed me from this fight was someone familiar to me – Angel Marrero – a local professional boxer.

Angel confronted me, "You think you're tough? You like to fight?" I quickly responded in a cocky tone, "Yeah, so what." Angel challenged me to meet him the following day in front of Figueroa's Market, the neighborhood bodega, at five o'clock to prove how tough I was. Because he issued this challenge in front of my friends and peers, I had to accept. The next day, Angel picked me up in front of the bodega and we were off to the AM/PRO Gym in Allentown, a neighboring city. As we walked up the stairs to the second-floor gym, the sounds and the smell took hold of me. I spent the next two-and-a-half hours watching boxers in training. The shadow boxing, sparring, heavy bag and speed-bag sessions, along with the sit-ups, were all part of a well-structured and disciplined routine. It was a far cry from what I was accustomed to as a street fighter.

The next day, I was back at the gym. This time, I wasn't an observer but an amateur boxer in training. I was eager to get into the ring for a sparring session and show my stuff. However, the man who would become my trainer, Sonny, made it clear that I was not getting into the ring until he was convinced that I was ready – ready to be a boxer. This meant day after day, week after week of training and learning, without actually punching someone or being punched. The training was all about mechanics, structure and discipline, everything I lacked. I was 15 years old, and for the first time in seven years, I was clean and sober for more than a week or two at a time.

Actually, Angel made the rules clear to me after my first night at the gym – no drinking, no drugs and no street fighting, unless I had no alternative but to protect myself. He told me if I wasn't willing to take training and boxing seriously, I should not embarrass him and disrespect the sport. I told Angel, "Don't worry, I want to do this." The fact is, I knew I needed it.

My training began at 6:00 a.m. with a three-mile run. Later in the day, I would arrive at the gym with Angel at about 5:30 p.m. and spend the next two-and-a-half hours pushing myself to become physically and mentally tougher.

After about five weeks of preparation, Sonny said I had earned the right to get into the ring for a sparring session. By this time, I realized there was a huge difference between trading punches on the streets and trading punches in the ring. The streets are about being undisciplined, destructive, reckless and angry. The ring is about structure, discipline, preparedness, and – most of all – respect.

Four months after I started training – after countless hours of road work, ring work, sparring sessions, pounding the heavy bag, jumping rope and thousands of sit-ups and other body work – I was ready for competition. I made my boxing debut at the 1980 Pennsylvania Golden Gloves Tournament as one of 16 fighters competing for the welterweight title. My first bout was one of my most exciting and satisfying.

During the first round, as my opponent and I met at the center of the ring and traded punches, I caught a hard right that sent me into the ropes (at least that's what I'm told). I didn't actually see the punch, nor do I remember being against the ropes. What I do remember is standing in front of the referee as he starred into my eyes yelling, "Six, seven, eight." I recognized that I just received a standing eight count. I only wondered what happened to one, two, three, four and five. Did the referee start the count at six? No, he didn't. I was just "out on my feet" with my eyes spinning in my head.

What happened next is very clear. After assuring the referee that I was ready to continue, I looked across the ring and was overcome with a feeling of confidence unlike any I had ever felt before. At that moment, I knew that I was going to win the fight. As the fight resumed, I didn't wait for my opponent to come to me. I wanted him to know I was not intimidated or retreating in any way. Seconds after "having my bell rung," I became the aggressor. We finished the round battling toe-to-toe in the center of the ring. After a one-minute rest between rounds, where I tried to breathe in as much "smelling sauce" as I could, we were at it again. Round two was simply a slugfest. Finally, during round three, after giving and taking several hundred punches, my opponent went down and the referee pulled me back. This time, he didn't bother to count; he just simply waved the fight over. It was a knockout, a KO. This fight – my first – was the toughest and most exciting of the four fights I would have to win during the two-week tournament to win the Pennsylvania Golden Gloves, Northeast District, Welterweight Championship.

One month later, I was in Atlantic City to fight for the regional championship. This time I was not so fortunate. Given my style – meet at the center of the ring and let the best fighter be the last one standing – it was just a matter of who would land the big punch first. Although I was standing at the end of the fight – because I stood up after being knocked down to one knee – the referee had counted to eight. This time, I didn't hear any of the numbers being counted or any of the questions he asked. Instinct and conditioning brought me to my feet. The fact that the referee stopped the fight, even though I was standing, demonstrates the training and expertise that enables a referee to ensure a boxer's safety. If the fight had continued, I could have been seriously hurt.

During a brief break from the ring for safety precautions, I continued with my conditioning and looked forward to getting back into the ring. Soon, I was sparring again and participating in under-card and exhibitions during professional bouts and club fights. What I really looked forward to and trained for was a return to the Golden Gloves. Unfortunately, I started to feel significant pain in my right knee during my training. My reaction was to wrap it tighter and continue. During a morning run, I misstepped on a curb and my knee gave out again. This time, I knew the damage was serious.

Prior to the modern MRI and arthroscopic surgery procedures that diagnose and repair meniscus tears, the procedure consisted of open surgery and a five- to six-day hospital stay. I was diagnosed with a meniscus tear of 80% and severe multiple ligament sprains. While the surgery went well, the recovery led to a relapse. The morphine that I was given for pain was powerful and overwhelming, and the doctor said I could receive an injection every four hours. By the second day, I was like a lab rat, tapping the button constantly to get more, more, more. I entered the hospital as a very well-conditioned athlete with an injury. I left eager to get high. Being totally clean and sober for over 18 months meant nothing. The monster, the boogeyman, the addict that had been dormant within me had been awakened from hibernation.

For the next month, I was constantly high, even during school. I resumed my routine of smoking pot, popping pills and drinking as if it was never interrupted. One rainy day, about a month after my surgery, I was with some friends at the park, getting high and taking turns riding a stolen dirt bike. As I took a ride, I tried to leave the path and climb onto a higher bank. When I started the climb, the front wheel went up in the air and my right hand came off of the handle. Grabbing for the handle, I inadvertently accelerated the motorcycle and closely avoided hitting a tree head on. Unfortunately, there wasn't enough room for my knee to clear the tree. The motorcycle continued forward while I fell about five feet back. The pain was tremendous.

After yelling in pain for a few minutes, I mounted the motorcycle and rode back to my friends. I quickly left and dragged my leg on the trip home. A neighbor drove my mom and me to the hospital. While my knee was fine, the pressure from the impact traveled down my leg, shot back up because my foot was on the pedal and exploded in my Achilles. The pain from the Achilles injury was worse than the knee surgery. The doctor sent me home with a prescription for painkillers and several refills.

My goal of returning to the Golden Gloves was gone. Another fighter didn't take it away. It slowly disappeared through the haze of an injury, surgery, drugs and a second injury, followed by even more drugs. My knee and Achilles both healed within six months, but that healing could not compare to the collapse I experienced. The eagerness I felt to train less than a year before was replaced with an eagerness to get high.

Even though I would go off to college two years later, I spent the next 10 years under the influence. As a criminal justice major, my drug use stopped during college because I didn't want to be a hypocrite. Instead, I kept on drinking, drinking and drinking. When I finally bottomed out at the age of 26, I was sick and tired of being sick and tired. That's when I sobered up – doing it cold turkey.

A few years earlier, I'd started running again. As I pursued sobriety, running became my therapy. Now, 17 years into sobriety, I know that I cannot tempt the monster, the boogeyman, and the addict that are dormant within me. Even after 17 years, I understand that I am only one misstep from falling back into the destructive realities of addiction. However, I feel very confident and secure in my sobriety.

As a parent, I understand the devastating legacy of addiction in my family. Substance abuse has also been prevalent in my wife's family. I suspect, and many experts would agree, that some type of substance abuse impacts most families. Therefore, understanding substance abuse and addiction is very important for all parents. At the very least, parents should know that addiction is a lifetime condition and it is not something anyone can handle or control in moderation.

Therapy may include participating in productive hobbies or activities that engage the individual and deliver a sense of accomplishment. For me, boxing introduced me to physical training and conditioning. Although I have not stepped into a boxing ring in many years, I still work out regularly and enjoy hitting the heavy bag. In fact, I have one hanging on my back porch.

I am no longer fighting mad. I no longer seek to beat up others, or myself for that matter. Boxing helped me find my therapy. Writing has also been good therapy. To those who continue to fight others – friends, peers, parents, or other relatives – or beat themselves up with substance abuse, I encourage you to find an alternative that works for you.

Any structured sport, athletic or recreational activity, fine or performing art that provides this type of discipline for our adolescents and teenagers is worthy of parental and community support. Sometimes, the activities that our young people are interested in are misunderstood. Because of this, they go unsupported. This has been the case for boxing in my community. As I mentioned, I had to travel to a neighboring city to train and compete as an amateur boxer. Now, over 25 years later, as gangs become more entrenched, youth crime and violence continues to increase and homicides hit record levels, political leaders continue to resist.

Recently, the city of Bethlehem hired a youth athletics coordinator to work directly with youth in a predominantly low-income minority community. When the coordinator conducted an interest survey of older teens, there was overwhelming interest in a community-based boxing club. Well-qualified organizations and individuals came forward with detailed plans, offering to operate and manage the facility. Still, there's been no support from our elected officials.

I wonder how many of those young people who expressed an interest in boxing went on to join gangs, committing crimes and violent acts after their solicited input was disregarded.

Meanwhile, the AM/PRO gym and the other boxing clubs that redirected and remolded angry young men into structured and disciplined individuals have long since closed from lack of support. Entrenched youth gangs, an increase in youth crime and violence, and a record homicide rate followed.

Apparently, those who join gangs and are otherwise involved in crime and violence are fighting mad. Without viable alternatives of interest to them, these individuals will continue to engage in self-limiting, self-damaging, antisocial and illegal activities that not only place them in harm's way, but put all of us at-risk as well.

Note: On Saturday June 2, 2007, The Bethlehem Boxing Club opened its doors. This was made possible after two years of presentations and endless lobbying to community-based organizations and elected officials for support. In the end, it was the Council of Spanish Speaking Organizations of the Lehigh

Valley that trusted my judgment and my endorsement of this USA Boxing affiliated club and its representatives, which allowed for this opportunity to be realized. Judging by the first day, this club will certainly have a positive impact on the community and the lives of the young people who will train at the gym. Since I'll be a regular at the gym, I've already selected a locker.

Having My Baby

The memory is as clear and vivid as any I can recall from my teenage years. As I stared into the bathroom mirror, after a recent breakup with a girlfriend, I began to feel the stress and anxiety of wanting and needing to father a child. Many of the guys I grew up with had already fathered a child. There I was, 17 years old and I still hadn't. I remember feeling that time was running out.

It was common in my neighborhood for teenagers to have children. It wasn't that we didn't know about birth control. For us, having a child was a choice, not an accident. Many of my friends had children as early as junior high school – when they were 14 to16 years old. At 17, I was getting old by the standards of my subculture. Two years later, at the advanced age of 19, I finally fathered a child.

Although I had stepped out of the boundaries of my subculture by attending college, I did not escape the many social factors and experiences that influenced me and contributed to who I was, or at least who my subculture told me I should be.

I could not avoid the internal pressure or desire to father a child. As a college sophomore, having a child proved to be very difficult. For my best friend Milly, having a child as a female college student proved to be overwhelming. Like me, she got caught up in the expectations of our subculture. Unfortunately, as the childbearing partner, she did not have the support she needed to help her remain in school after the birth of her child. It bothered me to see Milly leave college. As her friend, I wanted the best for her. I also recognized that she was a bright, articulate and talented individual. She was also young and attractive, which brought on the suitors. Eventually she got caught in the cycle.

As I tried to manage the impact of this cycle myself, being both a parent and a student made me contemplate leaving school. I considered taking a semester off so that I could get a full-time job and save some money to hold us over financially until I graduated. Thankfully, I didn't. Somehow, I knew that if I left school, I would not return. Since my wife was the primary caretaker of our son, I had more flexibility to manage my two part-time jobs and my academic responsibilities, along with my responsibilities at home.

Unfortunately, Milly was faced with the responsibility of caring for her son without the support of her baby's father. This is a far-too-common occurrence for many young unwed mothers. And it's often the case for many females who choose to have a child while still attending junior high, high school, or college. The idea that one can master both worlds – parent and student – is more a fantasy than a dream or an expectation.

Although this is a cyclical problem in many low-income minority communities – both black and Latino – with warning signs and obstacles clearly evident, many young people from these neighborhoods continue to make the choice to become parents. Some are seeking to fill a void in their lives, other believe they have found love and want to solidify the relationship with a child, some just think it's cool, and others are angry with their parents and want to prove they can be better parents than their parents. The guilt/anger factor that defines the relationship between teenagers and parents in many dysfunctional families (described in Section II) contributes to this.

On those occasions when pregnancies are not planned, when they're the result of careless, hasty or spontaneous behavior, most mothers-to-be from these communities choose to have the baby. Having an abortion is rarely a consideration and is not thought of as a common option.

Note: On May 19, 2007, Milly's son, Sammy, graduated from DeSales University (Center Valley, PA.) with a bachelor's degree in Film Studies. Milly was so proud as she witnessed this accomplishment. As for my oldest son, José Jr., he will graduate in December of 2007, with a bachelor's degree in Elementary Education from Millersville University (Millersville, PA.). Likewise, I am proud of my son and also of Sammy. Two young men that came out of the same disadvantaged neighborhood and went on to graduate from college. Two young men that completed college prior to fathering a child. Proof that expectations can be altered and the cycle can be broken.

Influences and Role Models

As noted in my own story, the presence of an appropriate male role model was lacking in my household during my adolescence, a factor that contributed to my own "strike one." Matters in the role model department didn't improve for me when I stepped outside and hit the streets – and that second strike was very ugly and painful.

Role models were hard to find. Roberto Clemente was a hero in our community, but most of us had already given up the dream of playing major-league baseball. We were struggling to save ourselves or trying not to self-destruct. I doubt that any of us thought that we'd ever be in a position to help others in need. Finding a role model in school would have been difficult, especially since I wasn't looking for one there.

Inevitably, I turned to peers and to those a few years older than us for direction. While music and fashion were very influential, they didn't have the clout they have today. The growth of media outlets – such as MTV, VH1, BET and others – constantly bombard young people, all the while promoting an image.

Since I was not much of a dancer, the disco era had little impact on me and the subculture also failed to affect many of my peers. The only exception was the movie "Saturday Night Fever," which justified my alcohol consumption, fighting, and my dysfunctional relationships with my female counterparts. Those who did get caught up in it were influenced by the music and lifestyle, which led to lots of dancing, partying and keeping up with the styles.

Funk, quickly followed by rap, became the music of influence in my neighborhood. Having both the music and the fashion was very important. The music was easily obtainable. We would simply record the songs directly from the radio stations or we would pay someone a few bucks to make a mix tape. Keeping up with the fashion, however, was not as cheap or as simple. While I was in junior high, I couldn't afford certain must-have clothes, like bandanas, khakis, carpenter pants and jeans. I solved this problem by stealing these items from other people's wash lines. As I got older, shoplifting became the preferred method for my peers and me to get the things we wanted – whether it was shoes, sneakers, clothes, coats, jewelry, etc. I was never arrested for shoplifting, but others that "shopped" with me were not as fortunate.

By the time I started college, stealing clothes and shoplifting were no longer part of my lifestyle. If there was something I wanted but couldn't afford, I did without. I also discovered that there was more honor in shopping at the thrift shops. This transition was brought on by a sense of maturity and a readiness to leave my anti-establishment attitude back in the hood. Unfortunately, many of today's teenagers aren't ready to abandon their anti-establishment, rebellious and self-destructive attitudes. Doing without isn't an option they are prepared to consider.

Today's music and fashion, along with the celebrity role models responsible for promoting them, have an overwhelming influence on our adolescent population. It's this widespread influence that keeps them demanding more.

I Wanna' Be Like....

Our children often say, "I wanna' be like…" and they fill in the blank with a name like Mike, 50 Cent, Kobe, Eminem, Britney, Paris, or some other athlete or celebrity. Maybe former N.B.A. all-star Charles Barkley was right when he said, "I'm not a role model." Although Charles Barkley was emphasizing that parents should be the ultimate role models for their children, he also recognized that many superstar athletes and other celebrities are flawed and should not be put on pedestals for children to emulate.

Scandal after scandal demonstrates that many of the celebrities in the public eye engage in anti-social, destructive, immoral or criminal behaviors. Although most of these behaviors occur when they're out of the spotlight, that doesn't stop them from becoming public knowledge. Far too often, the public and private performances of many of these individuals are either inappropriate or set poor examples for our children. Unfortunately, their actions influence children at an early age.

As a Little League coach, I regularly see countless kids stuffing their mouths with large wads of gum. They want to chew and spit, emulating their favorite major-league baseball superstars, who are chewing smokeless tobacco.

On one occasion, I had a player attempting to score from third base on a passed ball. As he slid into home plate, the pitcher took the throw from the catcher and applied a hard tag. As the pitcher turned and started walking back toward the mound, I noticed that the runner who had just been tagged was charging the mound, intent on beating up the pitcher. I quickly grabbed this eight-year-old would-be assailant, pulling him off of the field and confining him to the bench. After the game, when I asked him what he was thinking when he charged the mound, he responded, "That's what the baseball players on TV do." These examples are just the start of an escalating trend.

Are baseball players aware of their responsibility as role models? Reporters from the Tribune Company newspapers asked this question to players on all 30 major-league teams during spring training and the first half of the 2004 season. Seventy-five percent of the 534 players who responded said yes.

Carlos Beltran – who played with the Kansas City Royals at the time – stated, "As a player, you get watched by a lot of kids...and you know you got a lot of responsibility. Kids are looking at you. They try to be just like the player they look up to." José Hernandez of the Dodgers agreed saying, "Kids are watching a lot of sports and they want to be like somebody. You don't want to do something wrong and have kids copy that stuff."

While many players acknowledge and accept that our children view them as role models, whether they choose to be or not, 11% of the players surveyed just don't get it. Players, such as Jeromy Burnitz of the Colorado Rockies, do not feel they have any responsibility in this area. Burnitz protested, "Is anyone else supposed to be a role model? What's the difference between us and the rest of the world?"

Among the others, 12% expressed no opinion on the matter and 2% were unsure.

One year later – in the midst of the steroid scandal that caught the attention of a large section of our society – the survey results may have been very different. During the congressional probe, Congress expressed concern that steroid use by professional baseball players would deliver the wrong message to young people. Even the most resistant players would have to acknowledge this is a legitimate concern.

Getting back to "Sir Charles," I agree with Charles Barkley that parents should be the primary role models for their children. Unfortunately, parents operating under the influence of PWG are either unable or unwilling to establish the healthy boundaries, the appropriate structure and discipline required to establish a respectful relationship with their children. But that parental failure doesn't justify passing our influence and responsibility onto professional athletes and other celebrities.

Nonetheless, we should be especially concerned about the influence of professional athlete and celebrities who endorse or promote products, goods or services directed at young people. Since these individuals choose to be in the public eye beyond their professional careers, they should be held to a higher standard. Whether it's Charles Barkley, Michael Jordan or Kobe Bryant endorsing sneakers or a gangsta rapper endorsing an alcoholic beverage – image sells.

When The Center on Addiction and Substance Abuse held their conference in October 2003, it included a dialogue on the influence that gangsta rappers and other celebrities have on today's youth. The Reverend Calvin Butts summarized an important – but a frequently neglected – issue when he said, "What they promote sells."

As athletes and other celebrities collect their endorsement checks, they must be conscious of the products they promote and whether a product is appropriate for their young fans – even if that product isn't directed at them. They must also consider whether a product is affordable, especially if it's clear that it will appeal to the young and the poor. Often, impressionable young people will engage in all sorts of behaviors to acquire these goods, including shoplifting, robbery, and assault. If they want the status that comes from having a product, they'll even steal money or items they can sell from parents, family, friends or neighbors.

It's time for more responsible behavior from corporate America. It's time to look beyond profit margins and take a share of this important responsibility.

Keepin' It Real

Make no mistake about it – it's on. The hip-hop invasion – highlighted by its marquee trademark gangsta rap – is taking over our society. This invasion, which has captured the attention of so many young people, has many fronts beyond the music industry. The impact has been evident throughout the entertainment, fashion, auto, alcohol, and real estate industries. It's affecting all forms of advertisements and is having a large effect on the "Bling Bling" industry.

"Artists" – including Ludacris, Jay-Z, Ice Cube, P. Diddy, Nelly, Snoop Dogg, 50 Cent, and others – are seen and heard endorsing products everywhere, as they continue to use their status to further the invasion. Whatever the product may be, if they promote it, it sells. The temptation to exploit this invasion is strong, perhaps even overwhelming. Anyone with a product to sell, especially those directed at young people, have to consider using a hip-hop marketing ploy. The rewards often exemplify capitalism at its purest. The cost of this hip-hop invasion is nothing less than a decline in our social morality.

The Janet Jackson-Justin Timerberlake stunt during the 2004 Superbowl half-time show, generated the most controversy since Ice-T released the album "Body Count," in 1992. The album, which included the song "Cop Killer," triggered a storm of outrage and controversy. Police officers across the country came together to protest against Time-Warner, the parent company of Ice-T's record label.

The negative attention and controversy did little to put Ice-T or his product out of business. In fact, the controversy may have served to further Ice-T's career, pushing hip-hop and rap music into mainstream America. Soon after this controversy, Ice-T was starring in major motion pictures and went on to become a TV star, ironically portraying a police detective on NBC's "Law and Order: Special Victims Unit."

Snoop Dogg, a convicted drug dealer and accused murderer (he was acquitted of murder), used his criminal history to promote his 1993, debut album "Doggystyle," which rose to number one on the charts. This was followed by several starring roles in movies. Today, Snoop Dogg is mainstream. Ice Cube, Eminem and other have also benefited from the eagerness and desire of mainstream outlets – such as network TV, cable, ESPN and others – to capitalize on the anti-establishment images and lifestyles they promote.

A major selling point for these individuals is their willingness and ability to continue to push social boundaries and test limits. These behaviors appeal to young consumers, who represent the audiences that these mainstream outlets want to attract. In the process, these individuals have become role models for a growing number of our children. The invasion is on. As hip-hop flaunts its being-good-at-being-bad attitude, our children are being actively recruited. Pop culture and the hip-hop movement are taking over and corporate America is a willing accomplice in this "bad is good" sellout.

It's apparent from the Superbowl half-time show that we have become immune to the crotch grabbing, doggy style, butt slapping and groin thrusting gestures associated with pop culture and hip-hop. Had it not been for the body part revealed during the half-time stunt, the show likely would have passed our lower standards of socially acceptable behavior.

CBS and the NFL had fair warning that this half-time stunt was very likely to occur. After all, someone had to upstage the Britney Spears-Madonna kiss on a prior MTV awards program. The opportunity to upstage the Britney-Madonna kiss, especially in front of a worldwide audience, was simply too tempting.

We're left to ponder: Did CBS and the NFL get what they deserved? Did they get shame and outrage or did they get what they ultimately sought – a growing market of young consumers? Ultimately, it just may be that we were all PUNK'D.

Rap, Repentance, Reparation

On February 11, 2004, the *USA Today* cover story was "Snoop Dogg, The Ultimate Success Story: From Drug Dealer to Rapper to Movie Star." That story only served to convince me that Snoop Dogg is the same person he has always been – a selfish and irresponsible opportunist. Throughout his career – from drug-dealing gang member to gansta rapper, from his movie ventures to his current role as product spokesman for mainstream America – Snoop Dogg has always been about Snoop Dogg. He has continued to exploit every opportunity to get paid, regardless of the law and any social or moral responsibility, in a selfish manner without assuming any accountability for his actions.

As a drug-dealing gang member, he made thousands of dollars a week selling crack and destroying lives. His drug-related gang activity led to increased crime, violence, addiction, gang-related drive-by shootings and turf wars. Has Snoop Dogg ever accounted for this?

However disturbing this may be, it is more bothersome to understand that his drug-dealing days were only a stepping-stone to his rap career. The casualties he left behind only bolstered his image and furthered his career. His drug conviction and murder trial only served to rocket his debut album to the top of the charts.

As a rapper, Snoop Dogg preached to his disciples about smoking the "chronic" and drinking "gin and juice." He encouraged them to "keep it real," promoting crime, violence and the degradation of women. All along, as his Dogg-pound disciples increased in numbers from the inner cities to the suburbs, Snoop continued getting paid for his exploitations.

Snoop Dogg's rap career was simply the next step in achieving his selfish ambitions. Once again, the casualties that resulted from his irresponsible actions were of no concern. As the Dogg-pound disciples followed his encouragement to get high and "keep it real" all the way to prison or the morgue, Snoop Dogg moved on.

Today, Snoop Dogg says, "I'm smiling, but I'm not happy." Could it be that he has a conscience after all? I don't think so! He's just not satisfied with his career. Same old Snoop; it's all about him.

To portray Snoop Dogg as the ultimate success story is offensive and insulting to those of us who are left to pick up the pieces of the thousands of lives he has adversely impacted. Parents, educators, law-enforcement and social services personnel have had to counter his destructive messages for over a decade now.

If Snoop Dogg were really interested in dealing with his past indiscretions, he could put his career on hold for the next year and take the time to visit schools, community centers, detention centers, prisons, hospitals and drug- and alcohol-treatment facilities and look his disciples in the eyes and confess that he has misled them. But that's not likely to happen. This suggestion would deviate from his master plan – to become an A-list actor as soon as possible.

Another suggestion to make amends to those disciples and the families damaged or destroyed by the preaching of Snoop Dogg would be for Snoop to pay reparations. After all, he did make his fortune from the blood, sweat and tears of these people. Although his civil liberties – including freedom of speech – allow him to "keep it real" and preach a destructive lifestyle, there must be a level of civil liability that holds accountable those who abuse their civil liberties. Paying reparations, as a form of civil liability, could lead to a balance between rights and responsibilities.

If Snoop Dogg is serious when he professes, "I'm not that person anymore," he should be willing to give back the fortune that "that person" amassed at the expense of others. To claim that he is "not that person anymore," and continue to hold onto the fortune that person hustled, is hypocritical and selfish. Paying reparations, as a form of civil liability, would demonstrate repentance and the notion of being "my brother's keeper."

Short of this, if Snoop Dogg were to be considered "The Ultimate Success Story," it would have to be for the way that he has conned his way from the "hood," into mainstream America and into the penthouse. The same could be said about other gangsta rappers preaching a similar message of violence and destruction – all at the expense of a growing number of young, impressionable and vulnerable adolescents.

The most recent crack-dealer turned superstar rapper – 50 Cent – has capitalized heavily on his criminal and violent history. In his debut album – "Get Rich or Die Trying" – 50 Cent boasted of being shot nine times. Headlines about his proximity to a shooting outside a New-

York radio station may have benefited his second album, "The Massacre."

Geoff Mayfield, Billboard's director of charts, stated "Rap is the kind of genre where contrary publicity can actually help an album." This "contrary publicity" also creates prospects outside of the music industry. Endorsement contracts and movie deals are the big rewards for misleading our youth. In fact, 50 Cent made it clear, "I make more money outside the record industry... I generate opportunities with my music." It's no surprise that today's youth have taken notice of this trend and are increasingly looking at this path. The latest career choice looks like this: Drop out of high school, sell drugs in "the hood," get shot or shoot someone, get arrested and get a record deal. Be controversial, anti-social, and offensive, get an endorsement deal. Then make a movie "loosely" based on your life and get rich.

These rappers are sellouts claiming they are only speaking the truth. They resist any accountability by stating that they didn't create the situations they speak of – crime, violence, drug and alcohol abuse and the degradation of women. They claim to be "storytellers." The harsher the story, the larger the profit margin. Why don't they offer stories of hope and of what could be, instead of perpetuating the message of violence and despair? Maybe because those stories don't lead to record deals.

They're all very blatant about promoting a harsh image. It's right upfront in the name of the group, the record label, an album or a song title:

*Niggaz with Attitude	*Outlawz	*Public Enemy	*Terror Squad
*Ruthless Records	* Bad Boys Records	*Deathrow Records	*Hitman Records
*Cop-Killer	*The Chronic	*Body Count	*The Massacre

All of these titles promote a defiant and anti-social attitude, one that fosters the Being Good at Being Bad lifestyle that many of our troubled teenagers take on.

As I described in my own story, I have experienced and understand the adversity confronting today's adolescents. When speaking to these young people, we have a responsibility. We must understand that our messages will either contribute to a solution or contribute to the problem. No matter how much spin they put on it, "at the end of the day," gangsta rappers – claiming to tell a story and keepin' it real – are selling out our young people. They are part of the problem; they must be held accountable.

It just may be that the African-American community and its leaders will have to take the lead on this mission. They have demonstrated a propensity to stand up to social injustices and wield their political clout to hold others accountable. Their action, or their inaction regarding gangsta rap, can also be viewed as part of the solution or contributing to the problem. There is no room for double standards.

Is calling for financial compensation for "damages" excessive and inappropriate? Consider this: When Kyle Doss and Frank McBride (two African Americans) were bombarded with denigrating racial taunts at a Hollywood comedy club – which included the repeated use of the "n-word" by Michael Richards (from the TV show, "Seinfeld") – they sought reparations. As the targets of Richards' reckless attack on November 17, 2006, these individuals turned to attorney Gloria Allred to seek financial compensation (reparations) for damages.

When asked, "What do you want to get out of this situation?" by "Access Hollywood's" Tim Vincent, Doss replied, "To be compensated for what happened."

Undoubtedly, the use of the "n-word" should be considered inappropriate and offensive at all times and under all circumstances, including rap lyrics and comedy acts. To condone, support or justify the use of this word by anyone would be to endorse a double standard.

This is precisely what comedian Paul Rodriguez did when he said, "Once the word comes out of your mouth and you don't happen to be African American, then you have a whole lot of explaining to do." Comedian Paul Mooney provided a more appropriate response. After viewing Richards' racial outburst, Mooney admitted that he used the "n-word" numerous times during his stand-up act. He has pledged never to use it again.

As for Michael Richards, he has paid a price.

A few months later, another celebrity reignited the fire of racial controversy by uttering three words: "nappy headed hos." On April 4, 2007, radio personality Don Imus used these words in reference to the Rutgers University women's basketball team. His comments prompted civil rights leaders, the reverends Al Sharpton and Jesse Jackson to call for protest demonstrations, rallying an avalanche of support and media attention to have Imus fired.

Although Imus apologized profusely, CBS fired him from his radio program less than two weeks after his racially inappropriate and offensive comments.

In the meantime, rappers have been spewing this lingo, and much more, unabated for over two decades.

Imus paid a swift and financially significant price for his comments. His firing cost him $40 million – the balance of his contract with CBS. So as Black rappers profit from the use of offensive words and sexually offensive lingo, others that borrow from this "word bank" pay a price – reparation.

The only way to halt this double standard is to close this "word bank" and discourage any future transactions. Violators should all be held accountable and made to pay a civil penalty – reparation.

This double standard goes beyond a "word bank." It actually extends into a subculture. Consider the following editorial as food for thought.

On October 26, 2003, *The Express-Times* (Easton, PA) published my opinion regarding this double standard:

African-American leaders and civil rights groups are again demonstrating their propensity toward double standards and hypocrisy. Their latest target being the board game Ghettopoly, a game that closely mimics monopoly.

Ghettopoly uses a machine gun, marijuana leaf, crack rock and 40-ounce bottle of malt liquor as game pieces and crack houses and housing projects as properties.

Al Sharpton has stated that the game glorifies thuggery and drug dealing. Kweisi Mfume, president of the NAACP, finds it "disturbing that you would choose to promote and capitalize on such negative aspects of society that cause great harm to individuals and to the African-American community at large."

I agree that the game is offensive and promotes a very negative stereotype. However, it is no more or less offensive than the lyrics in most rap songs and the behaviors portrayed in most rap videos.

In fact, I would argue that rap songs and videos which promote crime, violence, drug and alcohol use and the degradation of women, do more harm that this game could possibly do.

The music industry and the gangsta rappers have been promoting and capitalizing off of their destructive messages for many years now. Maybe, if the African-American leaders and civil rights groups mount an on-going protest and boycott those responsible for producing and promoting gangsta rap, including MTV, VH-1 and BET (Black Entertainment Television), we could take them seriously when they protest and organize boycotts because of a board game.

It may not be too late to save the next generation from the anti-social, anti-establishment rampage of gangsta rap. But it will only happen if the African-American leaders make it a priority to shut it down. This would mean going to battle with the "artists," most of which are African-American.

Are these leaders up to the task or are they going to yield to a double standard?

Some recognized leaders and other advocates have spoken out against gangsta rap including Spike Lee, The Reverend Calvin Butts and recently Apollo Payne, a former member of the Bloods gang in Los Angeles who now works with young people trying to escape the gang world. As a guest on "The O'Reilly Factor," Apollo Payne characterized gangsta rappers, their music and their impact as follows: "When you're saying something that encourages thousands of people to go out and kill people and have a negative input, that's wrong...you have this music that's encouraging people to be gangsters...it just has all our young people going nowhere fast...creating some music to make your own self rich and you're hurting your community, you're really just doing a not worthy cause at all." Apparently Apollo Payne has now chosen to be a part of the solution. It's now time for other to step up to the challenge, because this is no game!

Note: "Musicians" representing other music genres must also be accountable for any actions that may promote or encourage destructive, dangerous, anti-social and illegal behaviors. For example, Panzerfaust Records, a white-power music company boasted, "We don't just entertain racist kids... we create them." Through "Project Schoolyard USA" this music company strived to promote hate. Apparently, they are no longer in business. Efforts like this must be countered and held accountable.

"O.G." – To the End

As Crips co-founder Stanley "Tookie" Williams was put to death, he shared one final lesson with his Crips disciples and all others affiliated with violent street gangs. This lesson was delivered as death-penalty supporters and opponents capitalized on his high-profile case to advance their views. As the whole country watched, whether we wanted to or not, "Tookie" maintained his allegiance to gangs. He made it clear that his loyalty was to the Crips and the gang culture.

Given all the media coverage his case received, especially over the weeks leading to his execution, it may have been difficult for the average citizen to dissect what this lesson was. However, for those affiliated with violent street gangs and those who study these gangs, the lesson was clear and direct: "Keep it real." This means: Thou shalt not show or express remorse for your crimes, no matter how destructive or devastating your actions may be toward your fellow man. Thou shalt not snitch, no matter the consequences to you or how helpful your information can be toward reducing the violence toward your fellow man.

Many of "Tookie's" supporters argued that he could not show or express remorse for crimes he did not commit. This argument was weak, especially considering that as his supporters advocated for clemency, they did not argue his innocence – at least not until clemency was denied. The fact is that as co-founder of the Crips, Mr. Williams is linked to thousands of murders. He is also linked to the culture of crime and violence that has taken over countless communities across our country.

Mr. William's supporters argued that he admitted to a life of crime and expressed regret and remorse for his role in the gang lifestyle and those crimes that he acknowledged committing. However, he was sentenced to death for crimes he did not admit to. A suitable response to this criticism would be that, 24 years and numerous appeals later, no credible evidence was ever brought forward to overturn his conviction. Given this, his sentence was carried out.

My purpose here is not to offer support or opposition to the death penalty. Rather, it is to express my concern for how Mr. Williams' behaviors, as a gang leader and gang denouncer, affected and will continue to affect thousands of young people. A growing number of these potential gangsters reside in your community, or may soon be moving in.

After his conviction in 1981, Mr. Williams co-authored eight children's books with an anti-gang message and worked with celebrities to denounce gang violence. He was even nominated for a Nobel Peace Prize for his work. As a result, his supporters felt that he was deserving of praise, recognition and a stay of execution. However, since the time of his conviction, gangs – including the Crips – have increased their ranks and spread across the country. So much for the power of books – at least in this case.

Instead of books and celebrity interviews, Mr. Williams had the opportunity to share with authorities the inner workings of gangs. If he were sincere about denouncing gangs and trying to prevent young people from making the same poor choices he did, he would have cooperated with law-enforcement authorities by helping them bring down the Crips and other street gangs. As co-founder of the Crips, he had first-hand knowledge of the gang's structure, methods of operation, criminal activities and systems of communication. This information would have proven to be a much stronger and more effective anti-gang tool than any number of books. However, sharing this information would have violated the sacred "do not snitch" policy.

Those who supported "Tookie" must now realize that although the man is no longer with us, his work will have a lasting impact on our society – and I don't mean the books. These supporters, including national civil rights leaders and celebrities, can best serve society by utilizing their collective resources to mount and sustain an ongoing and multi-faceted anti-gang campaign. Unfortunately, this is not likely to occur. More realistically, be on the lookout for t-shirts, posters, rap videos and other mediums that will be used to memorialize and pay tribute to "Tookie".

In the end, "Tookie" delivered his final lesson: "Going out," the only way an "O.G." (original gangsta) wants to go out – as a martyr – adhering to the motto, "Keep it real."

Corporate Drug Dealers

Parents of college-age students beware: Drug dealers are targeting your children. While this may not surprise you, the drug dealers I'm talking about are not your typical drug dealers. These dealers aren't operating elusively with a constant concern that the police are about to come down on them; they conduct their business in the open. In fact, I've seen them approach potential customers and complete their drug transactions as the police watched.

As the parent of a college-age student, this disturbed me. Most parents send our children off to college with warnings about the drug culture, stressing that they should avoid situations, areas and people prone to drugs. No parent wants to have a child go off to college and become a drug addict. However, these drug dealers are clever. They've adopted a marketing ploy that strikes our children when they're most vulnerable. They don't even fit the profile of your typical street-level drug dealers. You won't find them dressed in "street gear" with oversized clothes and jewelry and they don't carry pagers or cell phones. Instead, they are scantily dressed, wearing swim shorts and bikinis.

How do they operate? I first saw them at work when I accompanied my son's college baseball team to Florida for a series of games. On their day off, the coach took the team to Daytona Beach for a spring-break experience. It was there, among thousands of unsupervised college students, that these drug dealers were pushing their product. As many young adults engaged in traditional spring-break activities, including consuming large amounts of alcohol, the drug dealers were handing out their goods for free.

It reminded me of my days in the housing projects, where drug dealers gave away free samples to the neighborhood kids – marijuana, cocaine, heroin, PCP – all in an effort to get them hooked and create new clients. These dealers were making an investment they knew would yield a steady return. The only difference is that those neighborhood dealers were peddling illegal drugs; the ones I saw in Florida were dealing a legal drug – smokeless tobacco. Other items were being given away as well: chewing gum, suntan lotions and even condoms. However, the smokeless tobacco was the only addictive giveaway item, the only one that carries a warning label, "Warning: This product is not a safe alternative to cigarettes." Unfortunately, most young people took it and began using it immediately. My mind was quickly filled with thoughts of many cases of mouth, throat or stomach cancer. The dangers of this kind of tobacco use have been clearly documented. I don't take issue with this product's availability for purchase in stores; my primary concern is how this product is pushed on young people in an effort to create clients for life, customers until death, all for the sake of profit. Any product carrying a Surgeon General's warning or a similar label, such as the one noted on the smokeless tobacco package, should not be a giveaway product. Restrictions should be placed on the companies that produce, market and profit from the sale of this product. We should not tolerate giveaways that promote smokeless tobacco.

Here is a great opportunity for our legislators to pass a law, one that protects young adults from overzealous tobacco companies, while still allowing them to sell their product. Passing this law would not be an easy task, especially because of the power and influence that the tobacco industry and their lobbyists have with our elected officials. Unfortunately, those looking out for our young people are not as well funded or connected. Hopefully, a leader will emerge from among our elected officials who recognizes the danger of this giveaway practice, someone who will take a stand and halt it. In so doing, we'll minimize the number of our young people who will become addicted to this drug.

The War on Drugs Has Failed Them;
They're Still Getting High

The war on drugs began over thirty years ago, which was long before they were born; yet today's teenagers will become the next generation of casualties of this politically motivated disaster. By placing a law-enforcement and criminal-justice emphasis on this issue, as opposed to a social-health emphasis, the problem has been prolonged. Even a simple test using economic principles – particularly supply and demand – would indicate that the war on drugs (which emphasizes eliminating the supply) has been a catastrophic failure. Let's conduct such a test. It consists of one hypothetical question which requires only a yes or no answer: If we could somehow close our borders to drugs manufactured or produced in foreign countries, including those in South America, Europe and Asia, would our teens stop getting high?

If you answered yes, you lack an understanding of drug abuse and addiction. If you answered no, you're right.

Even if we could somehow keep drugs – such as cocaine, heroin, ecstasy, marijuana and others – from crossing our borders, our teens would continue to get high. So would adults, for that matter. Many would turn to prescription drugs; inhalants found in their kitchen cabinets and garages; domestic marijuana, methamphetamines, and other drugs cooked up in makeshift labs; along with a host of other domestically produced drugs.

So why do we focus so many resources, spending billions of dollars each year, along with using military personnel to fight the war on drugs in other countries? Politics and profits, pure and simple. The war on drugs has become a multi-billion dollar industry. It's an industry that continues to stimulate our national economy, as well as the world economy. This war on drugs has radically inflated the value of illegal drugs. Billions of dollars leave our country each year as the drugs come in. The vast majority of this money goes to drug cartels motivated by profits or others rooted in terrorism. Drug cartels have no interest in changing the status quo.

On the home front, the war on drugs creates jobs – the need for more police, more prosecutors, more judges, and more correctional officers. In general, the war on drugs provides job security for lawmakers, law-enforcement personnel and everyone within the criminal-justice system. In addition, the war on drugs has led to an explosion in our prison population. As our prisons fill up, we continue to expand or rebuild existing prisons and to build new ones. Michelle Holton, a former police officer in Palm Beach County, Florida, concluded, "Our tax dollars fund the fastest growing industry in the nation – building prisons."

Those who design and build these prisons, including architects and contractors, continue to profit. The prison business has also crossed over into the private market. The Wackenhut Corrections Corporation manages or owns 37 prisons in the United States. Promises to keep the prisons full lure investors.

The mandatory minimum prison sentences being imposed on drug offenders continue ensuring that there will be an adequate prison population to fill these prisons. While it's our lawmakers who create these mandatory minimum sentences, the burden of paying to house the growing prison population is passed to the taxpayers. While those in the prison business profit from the war on drugs, the general public and our youth continue to pay the price.

The war on drugs has been accepted and gone unchallenged by middle-class America, partly because it's assumed that the country's drug abuse is concentrated in low-income, minority neighborhoods. During a 2003 conference sponsored by the National Center on Addiction and Substance Abuse, the director of the National Institute of Drug Abuse stated that it's become a U.S. practice to "tolerate drug use in certain neighborhoods." Now that drug abuse is exploding within middle-class America, particularly among white middle-class teenagers, perhaps the middle class will demand that we redirect our efforts.

Recognizing the flaws created by tough-on-crime policies, conservative U.S. Supreme Court Justice Anthony Kennedy urged the American Bar Association to lead an effort to reform the criminal-justice system. Justice Kennedy observed, "Our resources are misspent, our punishment too severe and our sentences too long." The Justice Kennedy Commission was formed as a result of his observation. Its specific reformation recommendations include:

- Repealing mandatory minimum sentences

- Proposing sentencing alternatives to incarceration for those who pose a low risk to society and appear likely to benefit from rehabilitative efforts
- Providing appropriate programs – including substance abuse treatment, educational and job training opportunities, and mental health counseling and services – from the beginning of each prisoner's incarceration.

The only question is whether our legislators can demonstrate leadership by moving away from the popular tough-on-crime rhetoric and replace failed policies and practices with meaningful reform.

Focusing on the supply of drugs, especially from foreign countries, is simply a waste of time and resources. In addition, this model will continue to be ineffective from a substance abuse and addiction perspective. During a 1998 conference for retired Drug Enforcement Administration (DEA) agents, retired Special Agent Richard Amos responded to a presentation with the following questions, "Sir, if America legalized drugs, wouldn't we remove distribution of those drugs from the cartels? Wouldn't we reduce the size of our prisons and stop criminalizing drug users? We have used the same tactics since the beginning of DEA, yet you tell us more drugs cross the border than ever before and they are cheaper than they were in 1973. Is it not time to try different tactics? "His questions went unanswered.

Retired Special Agent Richard Amos went on to join a new movement within the ranks of law-enforcement officials, known as LEAP: Law Enforcement Against

Prohibition. Founded on March 16, 2002, LEAP is made up of current and former law-enforcement officials who believe our drug policies have failed. The mission of LEAP is to reduce the multitude of unintended harmful consequences resulting from fighting the war on drugs and to reduce death, disease, crime, and addiction by ultimately ending drug prohibition.

The only chance we have to reduce drug abuse and addiction in this country is to abandon the war on drugs – along with its misdirected focus on supply – and place a greater emphasis on reducing demand through education, prevention and treatment. Supply will never diminish as long as demand is viable.

Stop the Cycle – Legalize

As noted earlier, my experience with drug use started at a very early age. Smoking marijuana and drinking cheap wine was common among the kids in my neighborhood. However, we never expected that any of us would progress into "hard drugs." Heroin was the drug of choice for the neighborhood junkies. By 14 to 16 years old, many of my friends stopped attending school and set up shop "at the corner." They became runners for the local drug dealers. The lure of quick and easy money was too tempting.

An experience with one of my childhood friends – Junior - during my freshman year of college sticks with me. On a weekend trip home, as I pulled my laundry and book bag from my beat-up Chevy Vega, he ran over to greet me. Junior, who was a few years younger than me, wanted to hang out that night, go to a club, and party. When I told him I had to study and that I was broke, he told me to forget about my books and offered to treat me.

Junior was sporting all the latest styles – new sneakers, lots of gold jewelry and a big coat. I knew how he got them, but I asked anyway. Reaching into one pocket, Junior pulled out about $400, following that by pulling three bundles of dope from the other. I learned that he made the money in a few hours that morning. I also figured that he was using, since most of the guys who got involved selling heroin eventually became addicts.

Junior tersely summarized his life and then focused on me. "Yo' man, I quit school. Now I'm making cash. What you doin' in college? Be for real!" At that moment, I asked myself the same question. Who was I fooling? Does a Puerto Rican from the projects really belong in college? After all, I was not a college-prep student in high school. I barely got by in "flunker's paradise." As I looked at Junior, I wondered.

In hindsight, I'm thankful that I continued my education and resisted the temptation of easy money. But I can't help wondering if Junior and many of my friends would have stayed in school or found legitimate jobs if the lure of easy money hadn't been available through drug dealing. Sadly they just continued the cycle, becoming the guys the younger kids said they will never be. Addiction, crime, violence, family dysfunction and incarceration followed the easy money.

Would this cycle continue if drugs were legalized and regulated? I think not. In the following chapters of this section, I will expand on this position, arguing that legalized drugs would reduce drug use and addiction, as well as decreasing the associated crime and violence.

Street Gangs 101, All You Need to Know

In June 2003, *The Express-Times* ran a four-part series entitled "Losing Ground to Gangs," which included stories describing:

- How death is part of doing business
- Torture killings that shook a city
- Why inmates are reluctant to admit gang ties
- Money is the draw, but violence is the price of admission
- How gangs thrive in a world of styles and symbols
- Why young people are vulnerable to gang recruiting
- A mother who blames gangs for selling the drugs that killed her son
- Why gang problems are likely here to stay

The series detailed virtually every aspect of street gangs, from gang affiliations and rituals, to their violent history and drug trafficking practices. As a concerned citizen, I felt well informed. As an educator and a community advocate, however, I felt that society had reached a point where we had conceded the status quo.

Information regarding street gangs is abundant. Countless articles, stories, books, research and government studies have been compiled with no significant impact on stemming the growth and expansion of these gangs. *The*

Express-Times series even chronicled the expansion of street gangs into smaller cities and suburbs. Because of the abundance of material, I have chosen not to include a lengthy review of the many aspects of street gangs here. I have provided some "gang awareness" information at the end of the next chapter for your consideration. Since the gangs are constantly changing and evolving, information becomes outdated quickly. Since many of the small cities and suburbs where gangs are moving don't have gang units as a part of their police departments, relying on gang intelligence to stop street gangs is not the answer. Cutting off the financial resources that keeps them viable would have a greater impact.

I explain this strategy further in an opinion piece I wrote, "Putting Gangs Out of Business," which was published by *The Express-Times* in response to their series.

Originally published in *The Express-Times* (Easton, PA), June 12, 2003

Putting Gangs Out of Business

I followed your recent series on gangs with much interest. The stories were informative and captured the many different aspects of gangs very well. However, there was one area in which you fell short: Can gangs be put out of business?

Although some people, including politicians, may want to downplay the movement of gangs into our area, I agree that gangs have moved in and, under the current circumstances, are here to stay.

Regardless of gang affiliation, colors, rituals, signs, etc., there is one constant –drugs. Although the drug trade has been ongoing in this area for as far as I can remember (more than 30 years), it was never well structured or organized. The "corners" in certain neighborhoods were a "free for all" for dealers to set up shop. It was only a matter of time before the more structured gangs of the big cities realized there was an untapped market a relatively short drive away.

Along with this untapped market, there also exists a seemingly endless line of recruits waiting to be drafted into their ranks.

Now that gangs have moved beyond the "big cities," beyond the "projects" and other low-income areas and into middle-class America, we can finally get to real solutions. Past practices have not proven to be effective in putting gangs out of business. Gang intelligence, more police, more prosecutors, more judges, more prisons, and longer prison sentences have only led to overcrowded prisons and higher taxes. Our jails and prisons are full to capacity with low-level drug dealers and those guilty of committing drug related crimes. The answer is not more jails; we can't afford it.

The time has come to make some difficult choices. We must rethink our position on prohibition. Legalizing drugs, under strict government regulations, may be the only way to take control of our drug problem and put gangs out of business. This concept has been suggested before. Former Surgeon General Joycelyn Elders once said, "I do feel that we would markedly reduce our crime rate if drugs were legalized." This idea is shared by others..

I have spoken with many educators, social workers, and law-enforcement personnel who agree with the idea of legalizing drugs as a means to reducing the drug trade along with the crime and violence that goes along with it. Obviously, many people would meet this concept with fear and outrage. However, if we were able to move beyond the emotions, we would find that prohibition does much more harm than good.

As a parent, I feel confident that I have educated my children on the danger of drug use (including alcohol and tobacco, which are legal drugs.) I trust that my children will not make the mistake of using drugs. My biggest fear is that my children may someday be at the wrong place at the wrong time – school, a park, the mall parking lot or just sitting on the front porch – when a drug-related shooting takes place. As long as our streets serve as drug markets, we are all potential victims of the gang-related crime and violence associated with the drug trade.

For legalization to be effective, we would have to adhere to strict government controls. One option would be to make the drugs available through a "state store" system. In regards to marketing, we would take the extreme opposite approach to the marketing of beer: absolutely no promotional advertisements. The hundreds of millions of dollars saved on the failed "war on drugs" or even a fraction of that money, along with the proceeds from sales could be invested toward education, prevention, and treatment. Making drugs available through a government controlled "state store" system would drastically reduce the price of drugs, thus reducing the crime and violence committed by addicts in their quest to obtain the money to purchase their drugs.

Putting gangs out of the drug business would also minimize the promotion of drugs: no dealers trying to "hook" people on drugs in an effort to establish customers. Contrary to what many people may think, I believe that legalizing drugs, under a strict, structured plan would result in fewer people using drugs.

If we, as a society, are opposed to the legalization and government control of drugs, we may want to consider supporting drug testing as a deterrent.

Given that "middle class America" is a major consumer of drugs in this country and regular clients of gangs involved in the drug trade, an expanded drug testing system could bring the problem under control.

We could start by requiring that all employees working for a company, agency, or other employer which receives local, state, and/or federal funding of any kind be subjected to random drug testing. Failure to comply would result in the loss of government funding. I don't expect that this idea would get much support. The hypocrisy so prevalent in our society would fuel protests and cries of invasion of privacy.

The bottom line on this issue is that we must move beyond the status quo. These drug-related gangs are constantly finding new ways to not only stay in business, but expand their business into new markets. In the meantime, we "stay the course" in the face of destruction. The gangs are not our primary problem. Hypocrisy and our reluctance to rethink drug prohibition are our primary problem.

The time has come for a dialogue on the "effectiveness" of the war on drugs to begin. The political propaganda must be pushed aside and real solutions must be discussed. I offer four options for consideration and debate. Choose one:

1. The war on drugs is effective – "stay the course"
2. Expanded drug testing – tied to employment
3. Legalization under strict government control – state store system
4. Other – please specify

When I wrote this opinion piece in 2003, I didn't exaggerate my concerns regarding my children being in the wrong place at the wrong time and noting places like the park or the front porch. Unfortunately, children in these seemingly benign locations are far too often the victims of reckless shootings and stray bullets.

Tragically, for a family living only a few miles from my home, a case of mistaken identity brought the reckless violence associated with gangs and the war on drugs to their front door. A week before Christmas 2006, 15-year old Kevin Muzila, a well-liked eight grader at a Bethlehem Area School District middle school, answered a knock at his front door and was gunned down.

Three months later, 18-year-old Paul Serrano Jr. was arrested and charged with homicide. Serrano told police he was following gang orders to kill a man over a dispute regarding drug sales. Serrano went to the wrong house and emptied his gun as the door opened. As he ran away, he left behind another innocent victim of gang violence and the war on drugs. He also left behind a shattered family.

You may want to rethink whether you still believe the war on drugs is effective.

When we talk about combating gangs, we must consider the effectiveness of our gang awareness and intelligence information. On September 18, 2006, during the Gang Prevention Coalition of Pennsylvania's Northeast Corridor, United States Attorney Pat Meehan stated, "We are competing with gangs for the hearts and minds of young people...wanna' bees, those age 13 and 14, are the most dangerous...they have something to prove." He attributed a growing illegal drug market, a prison culture that breeds gangs, and the movement of gangs from larger urban areas to smaller communities as factors leading to an increase in gangs across the country.

This U.S. Attorney's comments were the prelude to a presentation detailing the gang problem and the Route 222 Corridor Project, a $2.5 million federal grant to combat gangs along the Route 222 Corridor in Pennsylvania.

The following information, provided by a Pennsylvania State Trooper, was also included in the presentation.

What is a Gang?

- Group of 3 or more persons
- Common identifying sign, symbol or name
- Engage in Criminal Activity
- Creates fear and intimidation

Why do People join gangs?

- Fun, sense of belonging, low self-esteem
- Status, companionship, intimidation
- Peer pressure, financial gain, protection
- Too much unsupervised time, unhealthy/violent home
- Born into gang life

Do Gangs Have a Structure?

Yes. The most common gang structures are as follows:

- Leaders – oldest or toughest of group with extensive background in crime, they direct activities and recruit members.
- Hard Core members or gang bangers – the most violent members and enforcers, they intimidate the younger members and show them what is required to show loyalty to the gang.
- Wanna-bees – youngest & newest members, they may be involved only on a limited basis. May be more dangerous than members as they want to prove themselves to the gang. *"Wanna-bees are Gonna-bees."*

How Bad Is The Problem?

- Most experts agree that the problem is growing
- Gangs are networking across the U.S.
- Most Police departments have an officer identified for gang prevention.

How do we know we have a gang problem?

- Groups of people acting or dressing similarly
- Increased violence / criminal activity
- Gang Graffiti
- Availability of drugs in your community
- Significant increases in the number of physical confrontations or stare downs
- Increasing presence of weapons
- Drive by shooting within or nearby
- History of gangs in your community

How can I combat Gangs?

- Monitor Children's behavior
- Encourage the boundaries and rules
- Facilitate communication between schools, parents and the community
- Encourage children to become active in school/community activities.
- Report gang activity to police, (i.e., illegal activity, graffiti, house with activity throughout the day/night, youth using alcohol and drugs, drug dealing, youth carrying weapons)

How can I get involved?

- Become involved in a community group that reports suspected gang activity (i.e. neighborhood watch)
- Work with neighbors to provide safe areas and keep them clean and crime free – removing all graffiti
- Support programs that provide kids with positive activities and communicate with children about their feelings and activities
- Encourage politicians to support legislation that would make it a crime to recruit your children into a gang
- Become active in gang prevention groups

Other law-enforcement personnel, corrections officers, and educators presented information detailing characteristics of local, national and international gangs. Identifying factors such as "colors," tattoos, hand signs and clothing, together with statistics about gangs in correctional facilities was also presented. How effective is this information in combating gangs? Consider what L. Louis Jordan, a gang and law-enforcement consultant, told a group of law-enforcement personnel and community leaders during a workshop held a few months later. "Three days is all it takes. In three days, I could get your child to join a gang."

Obviously, the gangs are working and moving faster than those trying to stop them. This is not the fault of law enforcement; it's the result of the political bureaucracy. The failed "war on drugs," a thirty-year effort, is a primary factor.

And Justice for Who?

Every morning, millions of students across the country begin their academic day by taking part in a ritualistic practice that eventually becomes second nature to them: the reciting of the Pledge of Allegiance. As these students stand side-by-side in our diverse society – male and female; white, black, Latino, Asian; gay and straight; poor, working class, middle class and those from more financially affluent families – they recite the pledge without giving much thought, if any, to the actual words they recite. However, when pressed to consider the contents of the Pledge of Allegiance, especially the final four words – and justice for all – they may question if or how the pledge may or may not apply to them and others. As early as elementary school, students may realize that justice is not blind or fair, yet they obediently continue to practice this social custom.

The Justice Department's Bureau of Justice Statistics reported that during traffic stops in 2005, police used force more often against blacks and Hispanics than whites. Blacks and Hispanics were also more likely than whites to have their vehicles searched and be placed under arrest. It was also reported that in 2006, nearly 60% of the 2.2 million people behind bars throughout the United States were black or Hispanic.

Our drug laws are unquestionably a factor in creating this disparity. One law in particular, known for establishing a 100-to-1 ratio for cocaine offenses, dates back to 1988. This law, a reaction to the epidemic of crack-related crime in the early 1980's, increased the penalties for the possession and sale of crack cocaine over the penalties related to powdered cocaine. As a result of this law, an individual in possession of one gram of crack cocaine receives a punishment equivalent to a dealer in possession of 100 grams of powdered cocaine. The possession of five grams of crack cocaine carries a five-year mandatory minimum prison sentence. It would take 500 grams of powdered cocaine to reach the same sentence.

It should come as no surprise that most of the people convicted of selling or possessing crack cocaine are black or Hispanic. Contrary to this, most powdered cocaine users are white.

Few lawmakers or people within the law-enforcement, juvenile justice and criminal justice systems have been willing to come forward and speak out about these disproportionate numbers. Doing so would risk alienating their colleagues and peers, as well as sparking controversy and a loss of public support. Yet, such honest assessments about crime and justice in America are sorely needed.

Northampton County (Pennsylvania) Judge William F. Moran willingly attempted to do just this. On August 7, 2006, while presiding over a juvenile court hearing for a 16-year-old white male charged with stealing over $6,000, Judge Moran made the following statement as he imposed a sentence of six months probation, instead of jail time, on a felony theft charge:

"This is a break, and I don't oppose it, but I want to make a comment to the family about this. This is a closed proceeding. Generally – actually, this would have been open. If the newspaper wanted to be here they could have been here, but in the juvenile system there are what we call white-collar crimes, which don't get punished as harshly as violent crimes, and there is a reason for that. No one was physically harmed. This wasn't a violent theft. This involved no threat of violence. So I think it is appropriate to do this, but I want to just comment because when I do these things and I can look out at the family, they are middle class, white, just as I am, and I say would the same thing happen if it was a black kid or Hispanic kid. So I want you to understand that you know you are being given a break, and I hope that everybody in this room would give the same break to everybody, but if somebody looked at this they would say I want to put him in jail.

People are tough and don't like theft and understandably so, but obviously the district attorney and the officer felt you are a fundamentally good kid, and I hope we would do this for everybody. It may seem like an unnecessary comment, but I have to say [that when] you look statistically [at] what we do with blacks and Hispanics [versus] what we do with white kids...the case can be made that we are not being fair to minorities. When you read these things in the papers about blacks, Hispanics and minorities, keep in mind you got a break. OK, good luck."

Initially, as I read Judge Moran's statement, I was somewhat offended. How dare a white judge talk about how the criminal justice system is not fair to blacks and Hispanics! I thought to myself, "What is he doing about it?"

I soon realized that for a judge to make such an honest assessment is in itself a deviation from the status quo.

It would have been easy for Judge Moran to simply "rubber stamp" the plea agreement crafted by the juvenile probation office, the district attorney's office, the police and the victim. Instead, he apparently wanted to impress upon the young man and his family that those stars do not usually align themselves favorably for black and Hispanic offenders. Although he may not have articulated it as well as he would have liked, he was apparently calling attention to the inequalities imposed on blacks and Hispanics. Predictably, after his comments, Judge Moran experienced the criticism that comes with making honest assessments. Unfortunately, it was the African-American community that was most critical of his comments. What followed were weeks of controversy accompanied by letters to the editor, press conferences and a town meeting.

Experiences like this could certainly cause other elected officials to "play it safe," avoiding the backlash that come with making honest assessments, especially on issues related to crime, justice and race in America.

Disarming the Dealers!

Be it political rhetoric, political grandstanding or just plain ignorance, many legislators continue to introduce legislation aimed at establishing mandatory minimum prison sentences as a means to focus on "the war on drugs" and reducing the associated gun violence. On August 29, 2003, Pennsylvania State Senator Charlie Dent announced that he planned to introduce legislation establishing a mandatory minimum prison sentence of five years for drug traffickers possessing guns. Mr. Dent stated, "The message of my legislation could not be clearer: If you are dealing and you are packing, you are going to be put away for a long time."

Mr. Dent aptly compares today's drug traffickers to the gangsters of the prohibition era. He is off target, however, when he suggests that media attention and a sense of "machismo" fuel today's drug traffickers. Today's drug traffickers are fueled by the same thing that motivated the gangsters of the prohibition era – money. Since money is the motive, new legislation – which is punitive in nature – will not serve as a deterrent. The very people that this legislation is intended to affect may not even become aware of its existence. We must also consider that many of those guilty of dealing and packing are minors – children between 14 and 16 years old. How would such a law apply to them?

If adopted into law, this type of legislation will only serve to increase our already overcrowded prisons, which will result in higher taxes. Our prisons are already pushed beyond capacity with drug addicts, low-level drug dealers and those guilty of non-violent drug offenses. The war on drugs has failed, yet state and federal legislators continue to introduce new legislation aimed at reining in a situation that plunged out of control long ago.

The concept of legalizing drugs must be considered. Legalizing drugs puts the drug dealers and gangs out of that business. Taking the drug trade off the streets means no turf wars or violent battles for control of a particular street corner, neighborhood or larger area. With no turf to defend, it's likely that these unemployed drug dealers will be forced to disarm themselves.

Our legislators must realize that as long as there is money to be made by selling drugs, the drug dealers will not disarm. Any legislation attempting to disarm drug dealers is doomed to failure. Such legislation will only result in more people being incarcerated and more people dying.

In Columbia, Dr. Gustavo de Greiff, the former attorney general of Columbia, saw drug cartels become more powerful as they realized obscene profits from the illicit drug trade. Despite the financial and human resources committed to the war on drugs, he observed that the high levels of crime and violence showed no sign of ending, not in his country and not in others. In response, Dr. de Greiff said, "In the end, the only solution is legalization, with regulations to control the market."

Must high levels of crime and violence be our fate? Unfortunately, as long as our legislators continue subscribing to the status quo, the answer is yes. What makes this more disturbing is that our legislators understand that the war on drugs is a failure. Dr. de Greiff noted, "I speak with many politicians, and many tell me that I am right, that legalization is the only solution, but they don't dare say so publicly."

Note: On November 2, 2004, State Senator Charlie Dent successfully completed his campaign to be elected to the United States Congress. As a freshman congressman, he supported HR 1279, Gang Deterrence and Community Protection Act, sponsored by Rep. Randy Forbes, R- VA. By this time, I set in motion a movement to promote change, if only on a local level, which I elaborate on in the chapter entitled "Basta Ya." First I offer a reaction to HR 1279.

Congressional Rhetoric On Gangs

Congress just doesn't get it – not when it comes to understanding the factors which lead to gang violence and what actions they must take to effectively address this escalating crisis. Even as Congress passed HR 1279, they continued following a trend which has yet to significantly reduce gang violence. This model – or any similar model - which involves getting increasingly tougher on gangs will not be the gangbuster that it is intended to be. Instead, if adopted into law, this type of legislation will only prove to be a budget buster.

This same practice has already led to the overcrowding of county and state prisons at an increasing cost to taxpayers. It has placed an overwhelming burden on homeowners, especially seniors on fixed incomes. Given this, one would think that Congress would take a different approach to counter the actions of these violent street gangs. Instead, our federal lawmakers have chosen to stay the course and "turn up the heat." The new twist involves a plan to lock'em up younger and longer – a new version of "Scared Straight."

As a parent, educator and youth advocate, I find the passage of this bill to be irresponsible and negligent. The legislation calls for incarcerating juveniles as young as 16 – kids only a couple of years removed from middle school – for anywhere from 10 to 30 years in federal prison. It's embarrassing that this is the best plan that Congress can propose to counter gang violence. Many teenagers at that age are struggling to find a sense of direction. They may be angry about family or financial issues; they are impressionable, lack leadership and are easily misled. These young followers, posers and wannabes, are easy recruits for gangs. Many of these young offenders have experienced failure in their homes, their communities and their schools. Having experienced failure in these three crucial areas, they are armed with anger and are looking for an outlet. Add to this equation, the propensity for these individuals to use drugs and alcohol, as well as the availability of guns and other weapons. This combination – an angry teen high on drugs with access to weapons – creates a soldier of destruction. Gangs, with the attraction and glorification of fast money, "pimped out rides," and a sense of belonging, fill the void for these displaced young people. For these individuals, the idea of serving 10 to 30 years in federal prison is not a deterrent. Many of these young gang bangers don't expect to – or don't care to – live that long. Whether we incarcerate them or they continue to kill each other, there will be no shortage of recruits. In fact, new recruits are lining up faster than we can jail them or bury them. Gang violence will not be reduced by this type of gangbuster legislation. In no way am I minimizing the actions of these young offenders. In addition to the destruction they inflict on each other, they cause real pain and destruction in countless families, communities, and in society in general. However, if we really want to bring about change, we must understand the factors that keep gangs viable.

Anyone who has studied street gangs must realize that drug prohibition is the major contributing factor to their viability. While this factor must be addressed, Congress would rather avoid the discussion. The cost of the getting-tough-on-gangs model will only continue to place a financial burden on taxpayers. Lehigh Valley, PA has already experienced huge tax increases at the county level, in part to fund a $23 million prison expansion in Northampton County and a $50 million prison project in Lehigh County. In addition, prison overcrowding has forced Northampton County to budget millions of dollars to house their inmates at other county prisons (less than one year after the Northampton County Prison expansion was completed, the prison was again operating over capacity).

At the state level, the Pennsylvania Department of Corrections reports that 16 of 26 state prisons are over capacity with more than 41,000 inmates. In 2004, it was reported that U.S. prisons took in 900 inmates per week, largely attributed to get-tough policies and mandatory drug sentences. With a prison population of over 2.1 million people, at an average cost of approximately $30,000 per inmate, it's no surprise that the United States spends $57 billion annually in our prisons and jails. Does this make you feel safer? Not if you listen to what Police Chief Stephen Mazzeo (Easton, PA) told a group of residents after an apparent gang-related homicide. "You've got real serious gang issues here. You've got real serious drug issues here… we know there will be retaliation."

We can do better than lock'em up younger and longer policies, gangbuster legislation and budget-buster rhetoric.

Until I'm in Congress, I'll continue to promote proactive strategies rather than punitive measures to address the crime and violence plaguing a growing number of teens. Jail or death should not be an above-average probability for these young people. However, as long as our legislators continue to subscribe to the status quo, they will remain indifferent to the lives being lost.

While countless examples could be used to support this position, I offer you one that moved me into action. On February 23, 2004, Billy Barnes was murdered. *The Morning Call* printed my thoughts on this tragedy in an opinion piece entitled, "As Young People are Killed, Inaction Signals Indifference."

Originally published in *The Morning Call* (Allentown, PA), March 11, 2004

As Young People are Killed, Inaction Signals Indifference

Grief, sadness, outrage, sorrow, anger, disbelief, denial and even guilt. These are some of the emotions shared during the funeral of a young man whose life was tragically taken at the age of sixteen. This young man was the son of two childhood friends of mine. He was also a former student of mine at Broughal Middle School and close friend and classmate of my daughter.

Above all, I remember a caring, joyful, friendly and very bright young man. He was quick with a joke and had a contagious smile. I was not at all surprised to see several hundred people, including family, friends, classmates, teachers, counselors and school administrators, come together to mourn this loss of life.

As often occurs when I attend the funeral of a young person tragically killed by violence or lost to drugs, especially young relatives or former students, I wondered if I could have done more to help. As a parent, school administrator and youth advocate, I am in constant contact with young adolescents and teenagers. I fully understand that it is a very difficult time of transition, a time when these individuals struggle for a sense of direction, a time when they can be easily misled. This is the challenge we face – saving our youths. However, the solutions can be as simple as providing more structure and discipline in the home, schools and community or as complex as lobbying elected officials to prioritize this crisis. Therein lies the dilemma, where do we focus our efforts?

Recent reports set the murder rate on the island of Puerto Rico, a United States commonwealth, at two people every five days. This is important to understand because many of the factors that contribute to the murder rate in Puerto Rico are evident here on the mainland – drug prohibition, gangs and violence. On the mainland, in large cities across the country such as Chicago and New York, the murder rate is over 500 murders per year. Closer to home, cities such as Philadelphia and Reading continue to struggle with their murder rates. Given that most of these murder victims are young, poor minority males, there are not many "leaders" coming forward asking questions or seeking solutions – inaction signals indifferences.

This became the topic of conversation between myself and another childhood friend during the services for the young man killed. Frederick Marr, III, a well-educated professional, was a Little League teammate of mine along with the father of the young man we came to mourn. As we watched the large gathering of young people, united by the emotions brought on by this tragedy, we discussed the many factors which contribute to these types of tragedies and possible remedies. We also recognized, scary but true, the next victim could be within our company.

As we discussed contributing factors, we immediately focused on our schools and communities – we focused on "the system." We agreed that schools must address factors which contribute to school failure. The dropout rate for Latino and African American students is unacceptable. We agreed that our elected officials at the local, state and federal levels must prioritize this crisis and make more resources available for youth related services. Education, job training, legitimate economic opportunities, drug and alcohol prevention and treatment, and health services must be on the agenda along with the reduction of crime and violence. The entertainment industry, especially movies and music that glorify drug and alcohol use along with crime and violence, must be held accountable.

The task seems almost insurmountable, yet the task must be taken on. If "the system," as the big picture, were our only obstacle, the task would be difficult enough. However, Fred and I know that the answers may be within our own communities. We must establish support systems within our communities to assist parents experiencing difficulties with their children. Our neighborhood centers and churches must be prepared to take on the responsibility. We must also step up and challenge the neighborhood hustlers that have taken over our streets and communities by setting up their shops in the illegal drug market. We know who they are and how they operate.

It just may be that the responsibility of saving our children falls on us. We can no longer wait for "the system" via our "elected leader" to look out for our young Latino and African-American brothers and sisters – every life is precious. We must recognize our faults and weaknesses as a community correct our faults and strengthen our resolve to protect our children. This means that in addition to holding the politicians accountable, we must focus on those amongst ourselves that are causing harm and misleading our children. The people causing us the most harm often are the ones that most resemble us. As we lay yet another young soul to rest, let's keep our promise to him when we say –your death will not be in vain. Fred and I have made a commitment to keep this issue at the top of our agendas. We also know there are many dedicated Latino and African-American brothers and sisters working very hard everyday in our schools and communities. We must come together, along with all others willing to help, in an effort to stop the violence, stop the killings. Rest in peace Billy – you will not be forgotten.

Basta Ya (Enough Already)

"Basta Ya" is a Spanish phrase that means "Enough already." That is precisely how I felt after Billy was killed. Having served as a board member for numerous community groups and several task forces, with little or no significant long-term impact, it was time to start an organization that could focus on the many issues contributing to the detriment of our youth and create opportunities for them to excel.

We formed CAPERS – Community Advocates Promoting Education, Recreation, Support – as the vehicle for outlining our agenda. We wanted to proceed without the political and bureaucratic hypocrisy that limit many youth-oriented community groups. The only concession made at the onset was the selection of the group's name. Several board members regarded "Basta Ya" as simply too abrasive and confrontational. They felt that we could accomplish our goals, secure the appropriate partnerships, and gain the support of the community by coming forward with a more inviting name for our organization. Developing our mission statement and identifying our target areas and projects was not very difficult, for two key reasons:

1. *The selection of the founding board members.*
   Each person I selected was directly involved with our target population in a professional or community-based capacity, was recognized as a youth advocate, could mobilize a group of

young people with little notice, wanted to make a difference, and was willing to invest the time to do whatever is necessary.

2. *Mutual understanding.* There was very little, if any dissension among us regarding what we wanted to accomplish and how we would go about it. We all understood that there was no room for personal agendas.

As will become evident, the majority of the focus of CAPERS projects is directed at minority – Latino and African American – students. This is intentional due to the lack of diversity in the professions we are targeting.

The following pages of this section describe the major areas and projects that the organization has begun through various partnerships, including:

- Encouraging minority students to become teachers at the elementary and secondary school level in the Bethlehem area school district
- Encouraging the recruitment of minority police officer by the city of Bethlehem
- Increasing minority youth activities
- Increasing the diversity of local EMT, fire, medical technicians and nursing staffs
- Support the anonymous reporting of illegal drug activity and other crimes

It's our hope that this model – which was our initial model – will serve as a template for adoption in other cities across the country.

Note: Since our inception in May of 2004, our initiatives, target areas and partnerships have changed slightly and/or expanded. However, our focus of creating educational and athletic/recreational opportunities for minority youth has not changed.

C.A.P.E.R.S.

Community Advocates Promoting
Education Recreation Support

Mission Statement

To work cooperatively with our educational, political and community leaders. To build on the strengths of our community and schools in an effort to maximize the potential of our young people and the educational and athletic/recreational opportunities available to them. To identify minority students for careers in specific professional occupations in an effort to increase the diversity within those professions at the local level, and to benefit area employers.

Initial Target Areas considered included:

- Education Advocacy
- Employment Advocacy
- Civil Advocacy
- Housing Advocacy
- Recreational/Athletics Advocacy

Given the wide scope and range of these important targets, we realized that we had to be more concentrated in our efforts. We also recognized that other agencies /organizations were addressing these targets as well. Therefore, we decided to focus our efforts in the areas of education and youth athletics/recreation.

Projects

- Partnership with the B.A.S.D. – Minority Teacher Initiative.
- Partnership with the City of Bethlehem (B.P.D.) – Minority Police Officer Initiative.
- Partnership with the City of Bethlehem (B.P.D.) – Anonymous Reporting Initiative/ Check-Mate.
- Partnership with area emergency services agencies, hospital(s) and Bethlehem Area Vocational/Technical School – Minority EMS/ Firefighter/Medical Technician/Nurse Initiative.
- Partnership with the City of Bethlehem (Parks and Recreation) – Increasing opportunities for youth athletics/recreation.
- Partnership with the Bethlehem Housing Authority (Parks and Recreation) – Increasing opportunities for youth athletics/recreation.

Minority Teacher Initiative

The Bethlehem Area School District's (BASD) Strategic Plan (2004) clearly highlights the discrepancy that exists between the professional instructional staff and the students in terms of ethnic diversity.

At the Elementary Level:

- Elementary school teachers are 95 percent Caucasian, four percent Hispanic and one percent black.

- The ethnic composition of elementary school students for 2003-2004 is 58 percent Caucasian, 31 percent Hispanic and eight percent black.

At the Secondary Level:

- Secondary school teachers are 93 percent Caucasian, five percent Hispanic, and one percent black.
- The ethnic composition of secondary school students for 2003-2004 is 65 percent Caucasian, 27 percent Hispanic and six percent black.

Although the Bethlehem Area School District has consistently made efforts to recruit and retain qualified minority teachers, including recruitment efforts at colleges and universities (in state and out-of-state), career fairs and recruitment efforts in Spanish- speaking countries, their efforts have not yielded a more diverse instructional staff. The CAPERS plan calls for recruiting from within.

* Recruiting minority students to become teachers –
Partnership with B.A.S.D.

- Select college-bound minority high school students intending to major in education (elementary and secondary education)
- Students will be provided a conditional scholarship, for four years, toward tuition.
- Upon graduation, student will commit to employment with B.A.S.D.

- Student will receive credit toward the conditional scholarship for each year of service – maximum of four years.
- Students choosing not to seek employment as a teacher with B.A.S.D. will be required to repay the conditional scholarship.

Note: Students must complete an application and meet established criteria to be considered for a CAPERS conditional scholarship. All students selected for the initiative will be assigned a mentor for the duration of their college experience. Matching scholarship partnership will be sought with participating colleges/universities.

Minority Police Officer Initiative

The city of Bethlehem also continues to experience a racial discrepancy between the department and the citizens it's entrusted to protect and serve. According to the U.S. Census Bureau's 2000 demographic profile for the City of Bethlehem, PA, the city population is 71,329. While Hispanics make up 18.2% (13,002) of the total population, only two Hispanics serve on the Bethlehem Police Department as police officers. That amounts to less than 2% of the 145 police officers on the force. Blacks make up 3.6% of the city population (2,596) and account for three officers (2%) on the city police force.

The discrepancies have a devastating impact on the community. Police officers serve in a position where they are in constant contact with the community. Therefore, communication and trust is vital to ensure their safety and the safety of the citizens. When a language and cultural barrier exist between the police and a significant number of the community, communication and trust is difficult to establish. Whether it is a domestic violence call, a traffic stop, drug investigation or a violent crime, the discrepancy that exists between the police department and the community continues to hinder the effectiveness of the police and cooperation between the police and city residents. CAPERS developed a plan to address these shortcomings in an effort to help diversify the police department and encourage city residents to be more cooperative and involved in the reporting and investigation of crimes.

*Recruiting minority students to become police officers – Partnership with the City of Bethlehem

- Select college-bound (associate degree program) minority high school students intending to major in criminal-justice administration.
- Students will be provided a conditional scholarship, for two years, toward tuition.
- Upon graduation student will seek employment with the Bethlehem Police Department – students must take and pass the police civil-service exam to be eligible to serve.
- Student will receive credit toward the conditional scholarship for each year of service – maximum of two years.
- Students choosing not to seek employment as a police officer with the Bethlehem Police Department will be required to repay the conditional scholarship.

Note: Students must complete an application and meet established criteria to be considered for a CAPERS conditional scholarship. All students selected for the initiative will be assigned a mentor for the duration of their college experience. Matching scholarship will be sought with participating colleges/universities.

Anonymous Reporting Initiative
*Partner with residents and community leaders to identify and report illegal drug activity and other crimes.

- Anonymous reports to the Bethlehem Police Department of all illegal drug activity and other crimes (Check-Mate Program).
- Attend block watch meetings in an effort to assist block watch groups in their efforts to rid their neighborhoods of illegal drug activity and other crimes.
- Promote the Check-Mate Program on Spanish television and radio.
- Provide Spanish language training to 911 police non-emergency dispatchers.

The community must be involved as part of the solution. Neighborhood residents, business owners and community leaders must report illegal activities, including drug crimes, gang violence, property crimes, domestic violence and any other illegal activity that perpetuates the cycle of failure. Without community involvement, the cycle will continue. Counterproductive practices – such as "stop snitching" – only serve to maintain a subculture ruled by crime, intimidation and fear.

Minority EMT/Firefighter/Medical Technician/Nursing Initiative

CAPERS also strives to diversify local EMT, firefighters, medical technician and nursing staffs.

*Partner with area emergency services agencies and hospital(s) to provide educational and employment opportunities for minority students.

- Select EMT, firefighter, and medical technician minority student candidates intending to pursue an associate degree related to employment in the service.
- Select minority nursing-student candidates intending to pursue education necessary to become employed in an RN capacity in the local hospital network.
- Student will be provided with educational assistance toward relevant two- or four-year degree program
- Upon graduation, student will commit to employment to an emergency service/health care facility for a specified period of service as credit towards the financial assistance.
- Students not fulfilling the required employment commitment will be required to repay the financial assistance.

Note: Areas of focus are EMT/Paramedic; firefighter, medical technician and registered nurse. Curriculum foundation is already in place at the Bethlehem Vo-Tech (Health Careers, Protective Services Clusters). All Students selected for the initiative will be assigned a mentor for the duration of their college experience.

Youth Athletics/Recreation Initiative

In an effort to maximize youth athletic/recreational opportunities, CAPERS has established a partnership with the city and housing authority recreation departments.

*Partner with The City of Bethlehem (Parks and Recreation).

- Park maintenance.
- Availability of fields.
- Creating more opportunities for youth athletics/recreation

*Partner with The Bethlehem Housing Authority (Recreation).

- Sponsor B.H.A. resident youth participation in local athletic leagues.

Through its initiatives and partnerships, CAPERS strives to increase the educational and athletic/recreational opportunities available to minorities. These young people must experience success in our communities and schools if they are to turn the tide of failure.

Section IV

Strike 3: Failure at School

Flunker's Paradise

It was the start of a new school year, teachers' in-service day, a day when most teachers are optimistic and eager to make a difference in the lives of the students they'll teach. As I walked through the parking lot, I spotted a bumper sticker that read, "I touch the future, I teach." It reinforced to me that teachers have an enormous amount of power – for better or for worse.

This in-service was held at the high school that I had graduated from 10 years earlier. While I sat through the in-service, I recalled many experiences at this school. I remembered the numerous fights in the parking lot or bathrooms, coming to school under the influence of drugs or alcohol, fond memories of old friends who have not fared so well, and a few teachers who showed an interest in me – none more than my photography teacher, Mrs. Dornbalsser. I happened to see her after the in-service – she was so proud of me and I was grateful for her.

The memory that struck me the hardest was my experience in Mr. Shovlin's eleventh grade Social Studies class. On the first day of class, Mr. Shovlin, or JP as everyone called him, stood at a podium wearing one of his many colorful suits, and greeted us. "Welcome to flunker's paradise," he said. "It would be impossible for anyone to fail this class. This class is dummy proof. I give group tests, open-book tests, and take-home tests. This is flunker's paradise."

Everyone laughed and some even high-fived one another. From the back corner, I remember looking around the room, realizing how familiar all of the faces were. Our teacher had just called us stupid and we were celebrating. Mr. Shovlin was our teacher – and he touched the future.

Insults – intentional or otherwise – communicated by teachers to students don't serve as academic motivators. This is especially true for the most vulnerable students – those with self-doubt. During his speech at the Pennsylvania Summit on Educational Excellence for Latino Students*, Francis V. Barnes, Ph.D., Pennsylvania's secretary of education said, "If you think about the people who have moved you the most, it's not the ones who have frightened you or embarrassed you. It's the people who have inspired you." This is true for all students.

---

* The summit is a cooperative effort between the Governor's Advisory Commission on Latino Affairs, the Pennsylvania Department of Education, and the Center for School and Communities.

Fear of Failure

Ever since I made the journey from flunker's paradise to college graduate, people have asked me what prevents others from doing the same. I believe the biggest obstacles are the messages the students receive from others and the fear that these messages may be true.

Although the messages may not be so direct, teachers and other school officials are still communicating to many students they are not capable of high academic achievement. The messages are both verbal and non-verbal. Since many students are coming to school with two strikes against them – in the home and the community – they're often pushing for the third strike - school failure – by misbehaving and underachieving academically. These behaviors are often met with increasingly severe disciplinary measures and decreasing academic expectations.

It's important for teachers and other school officials to understand why these students often exhibit self-limiting behaviors, academic and otherwise. Many times, what we observe coming from a student represents their need to preserve an image of being in control. They believe they are choosing to fail, taking on an anti-establishment attitude, when in reality they are giving up control. Since everyone expects them to fail, they are giving in to the negative attitudes and expectations set by parents, peer groups and even teachers. Their home life emphasizes failure, their neighborhood and community emphasize failure, and many of their school experiences only reinforce that failure. The hard fact is that schools are structured to educate those students who come academically prepared and motivated to learn. It's become apparent that many schools don't work for a significant part of our population.

It's important to realize that status is just as important to these students as it is to any professional, perhaps even more so. Having failed or feeling they cannot succeed in the legitimate culture, these individuals turn to being the best that they can at deviating from the established social rules – Being Good at Being Bad.

These negative attitudes and expectations have created a cycle that establishes the norm among many disadvantaged and disenfranchised youth. Those who deviate from it by striving to do well in school are often ridiculed and labeled as sell-outs. Those who rise above this attitude consider their high-school graduation as a major accomplishment in their lives. It shows that they beat the odds. But even among those who do graduate from high school, few are willing to press their luck by trying college. Self-doubt and the fear of failure are overwhelming, especially for minority students (such as blacks and Latinos) from low-income homes and communities. In most cases, these students have not seen many people from similar backgrounds who have blazed that trail and opened those doors for them. This fear of failure can be summed up as follows: If I try and don't succeed, it only confirms what I should have known: People like me don't go to college.

The safe thing is to stay within the comfort zone, to know your place or, as they say today, "Keep it real." It would be difficult to come back home, to face family and friends as the schoolboy who failed in college. Experiencing failure at home, in the community and even in school is commonplace. It goes with the territory. Those who don't make it to their high-school graduation have plenty of company. However, for those who do graduate from high school, higher aspirations such as a college degree carry a huge risk.

It's not "the system" that places these restrictions and limitations. The real obstacle is the individual's unwillingness to challenge and overcome the system. It's not that these students don't want to live comfortably and attain a degree of material success. They're kept from attaining those goals by the self-doubt and a fear of failure that they've bought into. A U.S. Census Bureau report noted that in 2004, adults with a bachelor's degree earned an average of $51,554, per year. Those with a high school diploma earned $28,645; those without a high school diploma averaged an annual income of $19,169. It also reported that 90% of whites had earned a high school diploma. Contrary to this, 19% of blacks and 41% of Hispanics were high-school dropouts. Since many of these dropouts are underachievers by legitimate standards, they turn toward illegitimate or illegal means to attain their goals – Being Good at Being Bad.

These students must learn that overcoming the system and moving forward in the legitimate culture will only be possible if they are first committed to overcoming

their own self-doubts and their fear of failure. I believe –
"life, along with the system, places many obstacles before
you. However, the most difficult obstacles to overcome are
those you place in front of yourself."

Dear Teacher

Overcoming the many obstacles confronting our troubled teens requires more than changes in the negative attitudes and expectations these students bring to school. We must also change the negative attitudes and expectations held by some of their teachers.

Early in my career as director of the peer-counseling program at Liberty High School, I was interviewed by a newspaper reporter for a story on the discrepancies in student suspensions. Although black and Latino students represented 24% of the student population, they accounted for 55% of the suspensions. At other district schools, the discrepancies were even more profound. When asked for my thoughts on the suspensions, I said, "When it comes to at-risk students, teachers do not always handle difficult situations as well as they could." I suggested that some teachers were less patient and less tolerant of students in need of those qualities.

As a result of the story and my statement, several teachers called my classroom or confronted me in the halls, claiming to be offended by my comments and demanding that I write a retraction. My reaction was to write the following letter to the editor:

Originally published in The Express-Times (Easton, PA), March 13, 1992

Some teachers help, others hurt minorities

In response to all of the feedback I have received from teachers at Liberty High School regarding the article titled "Discipline in School Intolerant," I feel that I have been given too much credit for its contents.

As a product of the Bethlehem Area School District, I am very happy that I had the good fortune of having teachers such as Miss Hassler (Donegan Elementary), Mr. Rotondo and Mr. Galle (Broughal Jr. High), Mr. Andrews and Mrs. Dornblaser (Freedom High) and others who were supportive of my peers and me. There were also teachers who often made us feel that we were less desirable – regardless of their intentions.

From what I can gather, things have not changed much in this area. We are fortunate to have teachers that work well with our minority "at risk" students and "go the extra mile" to make a difference in a child's life, but there still exists those who for whatever reason, make these students feel alienated and unworthy. I also realize that this discrepancy goes beyond our educational institutions. This discrepancy in the treatment of people is a societal problem. It is not my place to pass judgment as to which teachers are supportive and which are indifferent.

Our profession is strenuous enough when working with "good" students, but we are also called upon to educate students experiencing difficulties in and out of our schools, who may not always conform to school policy.

Teachers who strive to make a difference must continue to make the extra efforts because it will be appreciated (I speak from experience). To the others – nothing that I say will really matter. Only you know where you truly stand!

After the printing of my letter, several teachers objected and claimed that the letter did not qualify as a retraction. I responded that it wasn't meant to be a retraction.

One thing that I wanted to make clear was that I didn't think there was a school-wide racial problem. Rather, it was a social issue that each teacher should assess on an individual basis. The teachers mentioned in my letter were all white. In fact, there were very few minority teachers that I had contact with throughout my schooling. Those teachers who gave me hope, encouraged, and helped me to hold onto the idea of becoming a high-school graduate had very little – if any – understanding of where I came from. However, they were able to motivate me by demonstrating that they cared and expressed an interest me.

Communicating that you care about students fosters respect, which contributes to a positive student-teacher relationship. Student-teacher relationships based on respect, rather than race, ethnicity, religion or other identifiers, are more likely to result in positive student performances. Teachers who can inspire students to overcome their fear of failure and other self-limiting behaviors are truly the difference makers. As educators, if we are to inspire at-risk students and help them break the cycle of failure and underachievement, we must be fully committed. At times, this may require advocating or representing the best interest of the students, even if it puts you at odds with other staff.

In respect to race and diversity, I believe we are in need of more minority teachers, counselors and administrators in our schools. This is especially essential in schools with a significant minority-student population. Minority educators can serve as role models and mentors for minority students and demonstrate to them that all career fields and goals are attainable. This is not to suggest that non-minority teachers cannot motivate, inspire and mentor minority students. As I have stated previously, many non-minority teachers provided encouragement for me throughout my schooling and helped me reach graduation. Considering that I did not give them much to work with in terms of effort, this was quite an accomplishment. In fact, I was often working against them. I offer my junior high and high school transcripts to demonstrate this pattern of decline.

Broughal Jr. High School			
	Grade 7	Grade 8	Grade 9
Language	B	B	D
Social Studies	C	B	C
Math	A	B	C
Science	B	B	B
Industrial Arts	A	B	C
Music	S	S	-
Art	A	S	A
Gym	A	S	-
Days Absent	7	5	8

Freedom High School			
	Grade 10	**Grade 11**	**Grade 12**
English 10	D		
World Cultures 1	F		C
World Cultures 2	C		
Math	B	Withdrew	
Life Science	D		
Photography	B	B	C
Gym	A	A	A
Health	C		
Basic Communication		C	B
American Culture 1		C	
American Culture 2		C	
Clerical Skills		D	
Clerical Skills 2			C
Highway Educ.		C	
Problems of Democracy			C
Consumer Economics			C
Days Absent	26	52	60
Class Rank – 325/489			

As my transcripts show, my attendance declined considerably from junior high to high school, with further declines each year. Even though my academic program of study – flunker's paradise – was not academically challenging, my grades also declined during high school. Quite simply, I didn't like the school and didn't want to be there. Busing in a bunch of angry minority teenagers from a low-income community into a middle-class white school was a recipe for trouble. Racially motivated fights were very common. We fought in the halls, the bathrooms, but especially in the parking lot.

Twenty years after graduation, I attended my first high school reunion. I was one of only a few minorities to attend. I recognized several faces and even spoke with a few of the guys I had problems with. We talked about the fights, even though we couldn't recall any specific reason for them. The fact is we were ignorant. We didn't know each other and we had no interest in getting to know one another. We had attended different junior high schools and were brought together in a high school located in their backyard. Five years later, I attended our 25-year reunion. This time I made sure the group was more diverse.

By this time, I had crossed town to serve as an assistant principal at East Hills Middle School – the school most of my high school classmates had attended as junior high school students. What's ironic is that I now serve as the assistant principal to many of their children. Students from my old neighborhood are now attending East Hills as middle school students. Bringing together these two diverse student groups in grade six, when they're 10 and 11 years old, as opposed to bringing them together in high school when they're 14 or 15, makes a positive difference. As these students grow and mature throughout middle school, they are doing it together. They are sharing their life experiences and realizing they have many things in common. Bringing these students together at a younger age is breaking the cycle. As a result, our students, our schools and our community benefit.

There is still much work to be done, but we are now moving in a more positive direction.

As an administrator, I'm responsible for implementing a strict and structured district-wide student code of conduct. I've represented the administration in close to 40 student expulsions, most while I served as the assistant principal of Broughal Middle School with a predominantly low-income minority student population. This has been troubling, especially considering that if this code of conduct had been in place while I was a student, I certainly would have been expelled for truancy. At least 90% of my absences were truancies. There was no way my mother would have allowed me to miss 26, 52, or 60 days of school. Under current conditions, with school board members calling for a zero tolerance policy on fighting, an expulsion from school would have certainly been my fate.

Being involved in expulsions is not a responsibility that I take pride in. In fact, I consider each expulsion a failure, whether the student was expelled for possession of a weapon, drugs, assaulting a teacher or as a habitual offender of school rules. However, this number could have easily been two to three times higher had I simply "rubber stamped" every truancy, every instance of general misconduct, or every time that a student was late to school or late to class. Instead, I challenged the system and tried to hold people accountable – teachers, counselors, administrators, social services, probation, therapists, and others – in an effort to change the inappropriate and disruptive behaviors of these troubled students. Unfortunately, some students were too angry or otherwise not ready to be helped. Those that were expelled worked hard at Being Good at Being Bad.

My only consolation is knowing that other students benefit as a result of the disruptive students being removed from the school, allowing for a safer and more disciplined learning environment. In addition, most expulsions allow provisions for the expelled student to petition for reinstatement to the expelling school district after a minimum time period (which varies with the offense) if they comply with prescribed conditions. These conditions usually mandate successful academic progress in an alternative education program, individual counseling and other conditions set by social services agencies or the juvenile probation office.

Many of the students who were expelled from school continued on a downward spiral leading them to quit school. Some joined gangs or became involved in criminal activity. Others went on to complete the required conditions and successfully petitioned for reinstatement. Some even went on to earn a high-school diploma from the district. Afforded the opportunity to turn their lives around, these students overcame their own negative attitudes and negative expectations, along with other self-limiting behaviors and overcame the expulsion. They did so, in part, because someone believed in them and presented them an opportunity to experience success. Oftentimes, having the opportunity alone is not enough. These troubled teens need someone to believe in them, especially when they may be full of doubt. It troubles me deeply when people say, "It's too late" when referring to troubled students. It troubles me even more when an educator makes such a statement.

Fortunately for me, a teacher didn't think it was too late for me. One year after graduating from high school I continued to work at a fast-food restaurant, earning a little more than minimum wage. I was content, believing that I had maxed out educationally. On an early spring day, after arriving home from work, I grabbed a quart of beer and went outside to my spot. As I sat under the tree drinking my beer, my life came to a crossroads. A friend of the family, a teacher, presented me with an opportunity wrapped in a challenge. She stopped, got out of her car and approached me. She didn't attack the obvious, an underage drinker (she would get back to that later), instead she asked, "What are you doing with yourself now that you have graduated from high school?" I told her I had a job, a car and mom was happy that I had a high school diploma. What else could she expect of me?

Her challenge was simple – If you could be anything you wanted, what would you be? Without hesitation, I told her I would be a juvenile probation officer. I wanted to help teens that were getting into trouble, like many of my friends. Just as quickly she responded, "You can do that. You can go to college and earn a degree in criminal-justice administration and become a probation officer." Not wanting to be disrespectful, I didn't tell her I thought she was crazy. Instead, in an attempt to amuse her, I told her that sounded good, but I don't know how or where to apply to college. Besides, I couldn't afford it anyway. She told me that if I wanted to be a probation officer, she would complete my college application and financial aid forms. True to her word, she was back at my house the next day.

This is when my own fear of failure kicked in. Why couldn't she just let it go and allow me to be on top, having experienced what many from my neighborhood don't experience – a level of success in school. Now, she was asking me to risk failure in a world foreign to me – college. Not only was the concept of attending college foreign, my academic preparation in flunker's paradise was worlds apart from college prep. Simply put, I would not have attended college had she not believed in me; I would not have risked the possibility of failure. Not only did she get me started, she mentored me throughout college and has continued to be a mentor and a friend to me in my personal and professional life. In fact, she eventually steered me toward a career in education, telling me that I could still be true to my goal of helping troubled teens – that there are plenty of troubled teens in our schools. If I make only a fraction of the difference in the lives of others that Iris Cintron made in my life, I know that I'm reaching my goal.

Iris believed in me when I didn't believe in myself. She opened doors of opportunity and made a positive difference in my life and in my family. Thanks to Iris, I expected that my children would attend college from the moment they were born. I love you Iris.

Testing, Testing...

Teenagers turn to drugs because of a number of factors, including peer pressure, anger, depression, curiosity, boredom and the glorification of drug use by the entertainment industry. Because young people are constantly bombarded with many pro-drug messages, we must create and implement an appropriate counterattack. To be effective, this anti-drug strategy must deviate from the norm and not be punitive in nature. This may sound simplistic. However, deviating from the norm carries the risk of creating a political climate that is uncomfortable for our political decision makers.

If we are to put a priority on the best interest of our young people, we must be willing to push the comfort level of those who wish to adhere to the status quo. In fact, my experience has been that we must continue to push, even after being turned away time after time.

Student drug testing, as a proactive measure to encourage students to be drug-free, has proven to be a very controversial topic. Likewise, advocating for student drug testing has proven to be a very frustrating experience. The resistance of school officials across the country has deep reinforcement. After several attempts, over an eight-year period, to have a student drug-testing program considered in my school district, I stepped outside of my professional boundaries and appealed to the community by publishing an opinion piece in a local newspaper.

Originally published in *The Morning Call* *(Allentown, PA)*, December 11, 2003

Recently, I attended a three-day conference hosted by the National Center on Addiction and Substance Abuse at Columbia University. Titled Combating Substance Abuse in the 21st Century: Positioning the Nation for Progress, this conference addressed the most pressing issues related to addiction and substance abuse.

The conference sessions were moderated by nationally known personalities including Bill O'Reilly, host of "The O'Reilly Factor," and Charlie Rose, host of "Charlie Rose," and a correspondent on "60 minutes II." Other participants included the Rev. Edward A. Malloy, president of the University of Notre Dame, William J. Bennett, former U.S. secretary of education and the nation's first drug czar, and U.S. Rep. Charles B. Rangel, D-N.Y.

Throughout the sessions, two themes rang loud and clear.

First: Addiction is a disease and should be treated as a social-health issue as opposed to a criminal-justice issue. When addicts do engage in criminal activity, in an effort to feed their addiction, we must see the criminal behavior for what it is.

In most cases, the crimes are nonviolent. These offenders must be held accountable. However, the punishment must fit the crime. Handing out long prison sentences to addicts guilty of committing nonviolent crimes is counterproductive for our society. Less time in prison and more treatment while in prison would serve the addict and society much better. This practice would be most effective if it were applied consistently, regardless of financial resources or social status, regardless if you are Rush Limbaugh or the average Joe Public.

Second: Our schools are expected to take a lead role in the prevention of substance abuse. During one of the sessions, "Drug-free school: An American oxymoron?" moderated by O'Reilly, many of the challenges facing today's educators were discussed. Most of the issues were politically loaded, including drug-testing students as a preventive intervention. Drug testing (urinalysis or hair analysis) has proved to be very successful. John P. Walters, director of the Office of National Drug Control Policy, stated that among physicians, airline pilots and Fortune 500 companies, drug testing has led to a "better than 90 percent success rate for recovery. In schools where drug testing has been implemented the vast majority of students feel safe...as if they were wearing a suit of armor...they don't use drugs because they are tested."

It would be ideal if adolescent drug use were not an issue. Unfortunately, many teenagers are followers; they lack maturity and leadership skills. This includes athletes, honor students and students in "leadership positions" as well as the "at-risk" students.

They are easily influenced and misled. Although they know that using drugs is harmful and dangerous and they may want to resist, "just say no" does not work for them. Other means of resistance often lack foundation, are recognized as hollow and are easily torn down.

Student surveys, local, state and national, confirm the problem is real. In the United States, seven million people are in need of drug treatment and 23 percent of them are teenagers.

In the past, schools were reluctant to implement drug testing primarily due to ignorance. Most educators viewed it from a punitive perspective. The 1995 U.S. Supreme Court decision that ruled that schools could drug test student athletes did little to motivate schools to change their position.

In June 2002, the U.S. Supreme Court ruled that schools could expand drug testing to include students involved in a variety of extracurricular activities. Now President Bush has weighed into the battle, declaring that the Safe and Drug-Free Schools and Communities program has been ineffective. A change in strategy will emphasize student drug testing. This will include providing money to implement a program.

Sadly, we can recall the tragedies that resulted from local teenagers using drugs. However, these front-page headlines only provide a glimpse of the potential devastation. Joséph A. Califano Jr., chairman and president of the Center at Columbia University, concluded, "Communities that adopt drug testing would save lives."

As a parent, I feel strongly that parents should be their children's primary "anti-drugs." However, many parents are part of the problem. A well-implemented drug-testing program would be a great backup. Let's not deny our teenage population a program that will help them stand tall in the face of drugs.

The publication of this piece led to another opportunity for me to present student drug testing for consideration. Unfortunately, I was confronted with the same resistance.

A few months later, on the first day of school, tragedy struck our district. There was a fatal crash involving a car occupied by four students and a school bus. A 16-year old passenger was killed; another was critically injured and placed in a medically induced coma, while another suffered serious injury. The driver was charged with vehicular homicide, three counts of reckless endangerment and one count each of involuntary manslaughter, driving under the influence of a controlled substance and possession of marijuana. It seems that the 16-year old driver of the car, who failed to stop at a stop sign, was under the influence of marijuana. The time of the accident was 7:00 a.m.

Student drug testing is a proactive measure that can encourage students to be drug free. I'll be knocking on that door again.

Listen Up!

For the first few years in my position as director of the peer-counseling program at Liberty High School, I mostly listened and learned. I wasn't listening to other teachers or administrators, but to the students in my groups. The more I sensed an urge to offer insight and direction, the more I realized that these students didn't need someone else telling them what they should or shouldn't want. They needed someone to listen and occasionally point out options and opportunities, someone who showed an interest and cared about them.

These students all had a sense of right and wrong. However, this sense of right and wrong was often clouded by their views regarding what's fair and not fair in life. Many of these students felt they'd been given a raw deal and learned early on that life isn't fair. Many of these students arrive at our schools, especially our high schools, with two strikes against them (failure at home and failure in the community) and have drifted into self-limiting behaviors or into an anti-social subculture. Often their disruptive behaviors in school constitute a dare to school officials to issue them the third strike (school failure) and complete this self-limiting prophecy.

How do we foster an environment in our schools that will provide these students with a sense of belonging? By giving them a voice. Having a voice provides students with a sense of ownership, responsibility, and accountability.

Successful schools are able to establish fair, equitable, and caring environments where each student feels accepted and valued. Along with this, comes a higher probability of conformity.

With the growing animosity between student subgroups – such as jocks, preps, emos, goth, geeks, speds, skaters, racial/ethnic minorities and others – school officials must identify student leaders within these subgroups and give them a voice in the larger school community. On a regular basis, school officials should meet with members of each subgroup to discuss concerns specific to that group. They should also invite a representative to meet on a school-wide student committee. Although this sounds rather simple, a "no-brainer," many school administrators prefer to control non-conforming subgroups by utilizing a strict student code of conduct, zero-tolerance policies, or other drastic disciplinary measures. Other administrators govern with a sense of arrogance, a "because I'm the principal" attitude. It's often the non-conforming subgroups that get this attitude most frequently. Because of their insecurity, some administrators won't deviate from the status quo; they don't want to risk politically alienating themselves from the school board, superintendent, teacher's union or parent organizations. Others are so overwhelmed with the everyday demands and responsibilities of managing a school that they have lost their sense of creativity and optimism.

The administrators that are truly in control of their schools are the ones who give their students a voice, the ones who value what they have to say. The others only have as much control as the students are willing to give them. At any time, the unthinkable can happen – students shooting students, students shooting teachers and administrators, student drug-rings, and other incidents of crime and violence. We must foster an environment where students can talk to peers within their subgroup and to students of other subgroups. More importantly, we must listen up!

The importance of listening to students was reinforced by an FBI study. In 2000, one year after the Columbine High School Shootings, the FBI published a two-year study of 18 school shootings. Not surprisingly, the researchers found that the shooters shared certain personal, family and social traits. Most prevalent among those traits was the concept of "leakage." The FBI report defines "leakage" as intentional or unintentional actions that reveal feelings, thoughts, fantasies or other clues that may signal an impending violent act. Clues may come in the form of verbal threats, boasts, or predictions of violence. They might be evident in student writings or artwork. In most school shootings, clues were evident prior to the event. Apparently, the lack of a structured student resource or program – promoting communication – allowed for the clues and warning signals to go undetected and unreported.

A structured program provides students with a voice and an appropriate outlet to express concerns or troubling thoughts. This proactive approach can help to detect impending school violence and other disturbing issues. By participating in the peer-counseling program, my students were in a position to support and empower one another. They realized that they were not alone in their struggles and that they had the support of their peers. Negative peer pressure gave way to positive peer influence, as students developed positive attitudes and expectations. Although many of my students had academic deficiencies and were not college-prep, many of them made up for this with a newfound desire and a change in their academic work ethic. Many of them went on to graduate from high school and enrolled in community college or four-year institutions. Fortunately, before graduating from high school, they left their mark on the school and worked to change the school climate.

It all started with a roundtable meeting with the principal, Mr. Burkhardt. My students felt excluded from the decision-making process about school policies, procedures and overall school climate. Prior to this, meetings between students and the principal were limited to student council, National Honor Society, band, and other "student leaders."

The group was both excited and apprehensive about meeting with the principal, especially when they were told they had to set the agenda, including the topics of discussion. As a warm up, the students listed the basic issues – lunch menus, school cleanliness, and student discipline. Eventually, they went on to confront the principal with important issues, including racism, teen violence, drugs and alcohol, and teen pregnancy.

The end result was that the principal challenged the students to develop a structured forum to address these issues as a school community. They had become leaders within the program and were now challenged to be leaders school-wide. The principal was giving them a voice. The student's response was LISTEN UP, a student-produced talk show program, complete with media coverage. Panel guests and audience members included students, parents, teachers, community leaders, police officers, probation officers, health-care representatives and politicians, including the district attorney.

The following are excerpts and stories taken from newspaper reports provided by the two major local print media. I offer these to provide an objective and authentic perspective of my students' work.

Originally published in *The Morning Call (Allentown, PA)*, November 18, 1992

Liberty High panel tackles racism.

Nearly 100 Liberty High School students had come to talk about racism. That alone meant they were probably attuned to the problem and wanted to change it.

But when one of the panel members, Maria Gonzales, 17, looked up at her classmates, what she saw was emblematic of the overall problem.

Nearly everyone in the room, she noted, was sitting among his own ethnic group. Hispanics were with Hispanics, whites with whites and blacks with blacks.

Then she made an astute observation. What she could joke about with her Hispanic friends, she said, she could not joke about with her black and white friends.

"It's all right for me to make fun of Hispanics," said Gonzales. "But it's not all right to make fun of blacks or whites."

Sponsored by the school's Unidos/Peer Counseling student group, the so-called "talk show" was organized to bring students out to talk about their experiences with racism.

Taking part were several adults who are closely involved in community affairs: Angel Rodriguez of the Pennsylvania Power & Light Co., Jeff Davis of the National Association for the Advancement of Colored People and Peggy Amidon, of RISK, a student group. The moderator was Sis-Obed Torres-Cordero of the Bethlehem Action Committee.

"Racism exists everywhere," said Rodriguez. "It exists in the business world and everywhere else."

And for everyone, as well, said Jill Dunn, a white student council representative.

"It's not just whites against blacks; it's a two-way thing," said Dunn. "There are people in our school who are racist against white people."

Afterward, school officials said the fact that the forum was held at all reflected a step in the right direction, in particular, that kids from the different groups would get together to plan the event.

More important, said Principal William Burkhardt, was that minority students acknowledged that they had to place greater emphasis on academic performance.

"You're not a sell-out if you excel," said Elvis Rivera, 17.

The adults, meanwhile, urged the students to continue their efforts to sort out their feelings toward different ethnic groups.

"We've got to start to communicate," said Amidon.

Originally published in *The Morning Call (Allentown, PA),* December 13, 1991

Liberty students present anti-drug program.

The scene – two teen-agers pressuring a third to deal drugs – could have been played out at any high school in America:

"I can make as much in one hour as you make in a week," one student taunted.

"Just think, you can set your own hours," another one advised.

Then four Bethlehem police officers walked onto the Liberty High School stage, pulled out their handcuffs and dragged the students away.

It was only a skit, and the audience of about 50 people laughed. But the message the students were trying to deliver was very real.

About 60 of them worked for almost a year to get ready for Wednesday's "Listen Up" anti-drug program. The main event was a videotape they made, "Let's Stop the Madness: Drugs In Our Community." There was also a slide show, two skits and a question-and-answer session with experts and former addicts.

"We were tired of seeing the drugs in our community and the suffering," said Joann Rodriguez, treasurer of UNIDOS, the student group that put the show together with students from Liberty's peer counseling program.

Students were responsible for every detail of the 90-minute program, right down to writing and recording the songs used in the video, according to their adviser, Liberty counselor José Rosado.

Many of the students came from the counseling groups Rosado leads, and he said motivating them to take on such a big project was initially a problem.

"These are not National Honor Society kids. These are kids that have had difficulties at school, difficulties at home," Rosado said. "You tell them at the beginning of the school year, do you want to do this? They think they're too cool."

But he said the project built up momentum as he got a few kids involved, and they encouraged their friends to join. As the video developed, their enthusiasm grew.

"Once they are put in a position to look at something that's positive, their talents start to surface," Rosado said.

The result was a very convincing video that the students were visibly proud of.

Rosado started the video last school year with a $7,000 state grant. The students finished it this fall and put together Wednesday's program for its premier.

Rosado said he hoped to get the same group of kids to work on two more videos: one on teen pregnancy and another on dysfunctional families.

The drug video opens with footage of television news coverage of drug busts and murders, then shows interviews with inmates at Northampton County Prison. One of the inmates says that more than half the people in the prison got there because of drugs.

Students in the audience laughed when the video showed dramatic footage of teen-agers supposedly getting arrested for using cocaine. The Liberty students acting in the video were taken away in a police car and booked into holding cells at the Bethlehem police station.

Rosado's plan is to distribute copies of the video throughout the Bethlehem Area School District, but the students were realistic about the effect it would have in stopping their peers from using drugs.

"It's not going to make a big difference," said Arturo Robles Jr., "but it's going to open their eyes."

After the video, students heard a real-life story of drug addiction from former Liberty student José Pacheco.

Pacheco is now in the Hogar Crea rehabilitation program in Freemansburg.

At the same school where he once smoked marijuana in the bathrooms and drank in the halls, Pacheco said he got involved in drugs when his family moved from Philadelphia to Bethlehem and he made friends with the wrong people.

He said his addiction grew to the point where he thought it was cool to get arrested, and he was arrested several times.

Kenneth McGloun, also from Hogar Crea, told the students to be honest with themselves, and get help quickly if they ever ran into trouble.

"Nobody should end up like me, being addicted for 26 years of my life," he told them. "I threw my life away."

Originally published in *The Express-Times (Easton, PA),* February 10, 1993

Images of violence brought to Liberty.

A student-created video demonstrates the consequences of violence. A burst of light broke the darkness in Liberty High School's amphitheater Tuesday, bringing with it three startling images.

First, a young man with a huge scar across his chest. Then another young man with a cut on his head. And a third, lying unconscious on a hospital bed with blood pouring from this head.

As the photos flashed on the screen, rap music blasted from speakers. The music grew more urgent as photos of newspaper clippings began to flash, offering details of violent crimes in the Lehigh Valley and elsewhere.

The images and music were part of a "Listen-Up Talk Show Program" sponsored by Liberty's peer counseling program and its Unidos student club, which deals with social issues. The program's topic was youth violence.

The video, produced by students and edited by Unidos adviser and Liberty guidance counselor José Rosado, offered clips of students discussing a problem that has been invading their young lives.

The program itself also offered a panel of people who work with teenagers who have problems – a teacher, a police officer and a treatment center worker. And it offered two teenagers, including José Velez, the teenager with the scar on his chest.

Velez and his friend Arturo Robles told the story of how, two summers ago, Velez got into a fight that could have cost him his life. "I was looking for trouble," Velez said. "And it came to me."

Robles described how another teenager slashed Velez with a knife. "I kind of like flipped yo," he said. "I could see him on the floor. I could see his ribs."

Velez, who later received 20 interior stitches and more exterior "staples," said that even as his friend held him and helped him away, he wanted to return to the fight.

The program's audience of teens, teachers and police officers learned that Velez is far from being alone.

Donald Sabo, the Bethlehem Police Department's crime prevention officer, said that in 1990, city police arrested 848 juveniles and 212 of them faced assault charges.

The Bethlehem Area School District, meanwhile, is beginning to take some action. Assistant Superintendent Michele Kostem, who attended the program, said she's in charge of putting together a task force on teen violence that includes about 40 teachers, counselors, police officers, clergy, youth workers and other members of the community.

Rosado, the Unidos adviser, said he's hoping the program and the task force will make the community more aware that modern kids have to deal with all sorts of pressures at home and in the school.

Originally published in *The Express-Times (Easton, PA)*, December 15, 1993

Liberty program tackles violence.

The 'Listen-Up Talk Show Program' attempts to address a growing teen crime rate. In the darkened quiet of Liberty High School's amphitheater, Rev. Jesse Jackson anguished over the violence that's taking the lives of young people, church members stomped on rap CDs and gang members mourned the death of one of their own.

When the lights went on and the video stopped, about 70 students, teachers, parents, city officials and police officers found themselves grappling with the way those issues are affecting Bethlehem and the Lehigh Valley, trying to find hope in a flood of frightening facts.

The video, part of a "Listen-Up Talk Show Program" produced by members of Liberty's peer-counseling program and Unidos club, also flashed photos of gang-related graffiti that began appearing recently in Bethlehem and showed a television segment on the relationship between rap and violence.

The images and statistics provided plenty of fodder for discussion – and argument – for both audience members and six panelists.

Panelist Tulio Santiago, a Liberty senior and football and basketball star, said he thinks rap can sometimes encourage kids to join gangs and do drugs.

"I think it provokes it in some kind of way," he said.

Panelist Brenda Kramer, a Liberty sophomore who moved out of the school's alternative program this year, said she tries to make sure her friends aren't involved in gangs but she isn't always sure."

"They tell me no," she said. "I have to accept it."

Maria Robledo, who helps coordinate a block watch in the 1300 and 1400 blocks of East Fourth Street, on the city's South Side, said she and other residents are trying hard to keep gang activity away from their homes by working together and calling police when incidents occur.

Northampton County District Attorney John Morganelli linked the problems of drugs, violence and alienation.

"Twenty percent of our case load is just drug cases," he said, adding that another 30 percent of crimes in the county are related to drugs.

Morganelli told students he has little sympathy for offenders who claim they had nothing else to do.

"Quite frankly, I find that hard to believe," he said, suggesting that teens join school clubs or participate in Girl Scouts or Boy Scouts.

"We've got skating rinks, we've got movie theaters," he said, drawing snickers and groans from a few students in the auditorium.

Panelist Dan Bartley of the National Coalition Building Institute, who's acting as a consultant to local police, said he's seen the same problems crop up all over the nation and thinks that the problems can be solved, partly through acknowledging them.

"We've got a fantastic opportunity to be different than other places that have ignored or denied it," he said.

Other panelists agreed that involving the whole community can help solve the problem.

Sis-Obed Torres Cordero, an attorney and teacher who has children in the Bethlehem schools, said he grew up in New York City's Bedford-Stuyvesant and the South Bronx and knows how drugs and violence can breed.

"If we don't start working together, we're gonna lose this thing," he said, explaining that parents and teachers need to find a way to reach kids before drug dealers do. "If we don't compete with these people, we're dead in the water."

Listen up! Give them a voice, through a well-structured forum with the appropriate resources, and students will become involved in a process to address and resolve many of the issues confronting our schools. In addition to addressing the social factors, students with a voice will also develop a more positive work ethic, as well as a more positive attitude toward school and their education. Chris

Dunton, a colleague of mine while at Liberty High School, complimented the program when he said, "You can measure the success of the program by the things you don't see." Giving them a voice tells them they belong. Listen up!

Homecoming

I Still Feel Ya!

Time does not heal all wounds. At some point, the pain will resurface and be seen by others – even if it's 20 years later. As a student at Broughal Junior High School during the late 1970's, I was in the midst of rage and anger. These emotions peaked in October of 1979 when one of my best friends – David Sanchez – was shot and killed by his own father.

Back then I never thought that someday I would return to Broughal as the assistant principal – no one else would have thought that about me at the time. That's why my return to Broughal was so important to me. Many of my students at Broughal are mirror images of me at that age. Coming out of the same neighborhood and surroundings, I know many of their parents and family members. I also know their pain. I am very fortunate to be back, and I feel a strong sense of obligation. I want to let them know – I feel ya' – and give them a message of hope.

Throughout my first year as assistant principal, I had many opportunities to meet with students individually and in small groups. I always tried to leave every student with a positive message, regardless of his or her misdeeds.

During the spring of that first year, I was able to put together our first Homecoming Day. It was a day to celebrate Broughal – past and present. It was also an opportunity to share with the students that we all have obstacles to overcome, hardships to endure and goals to realize. Despite my position as the assistant principal, I was still overcome by my emotions, as this newspaper report demonstrates.

Originally published by The Morning Call (Allentown, PA), March 10, 1997

Broughal applauds its best. An assistant principal remembers a friend who died. Students are stunned.

More than 500 children sat stone-faced as they watched their assistant principal shed tears on the school stage.

At first, some didn't quite believe it. Then, they started whispering, poking one another, pointing out José Rosado's emotions.

Standing at a podium Friday, Rosado revealed to the entire student body that he's more than their administrator. Deep down, he's just like them: a product of Broughal Middle School, a part of the South Side, a bearer of tradition.

Perhaps, the children didn't expect such a solemn moment.

After all, this was their Homecoming Day, the school's first. It was replete with a 10-member student court that drew shrieks and wild applause as it paraded through the auditorium. Boys strutted in tuxedos. Girls shyly smiled in sweeping gowns. Proud parents beamed. Camera flashes popped.

The school band played "YMCA" and the theme from Jurassic Park. Cheerleaders performed a routine. The STEP team pumped up the crowd.

Successful Broughal alumni – such as city policeman Van Scott and District Justice Nancy Matos Gonzalez – gave words of inspiration, told the students they are who they choose to be.

Rosado, assistant principal since last year, was one of them.

Yet, 20 years ago, he couldn't have imagined it.

Back then, graduating from high school was an uncertainty, said Rosado. He grew up in South Terrace, a public housing development roughly two miles east of the school. He joined Broughal's football squad, hung out with classmates.

A close one was David Sanchez.

Sanchez also played football for Broughal, from 1975 to 1977. He wasn't the best, the largest, the strongest or the fastest athlete, recalled coach Michael Rotondo. But Sanchez, No. 32, had the biggest heart.

Sanchez gave 100 percent to the game and for his determination, he was named most valuable player in 1977, Rotondo said.

However, Sanchez "passed on" two years later, said Rosado. He didn't die, he told the students, because his spirit still lives in Rosado. Instead, he simply referred to Sanchez's death as "tragic."

Antonio Sanchez, David's father, shot the 16-year-old Freedom High junior to death in their State Street home in October 1979. The shooting left the South Side neighborhood stunned. The father was convicted of voluntary manslaughter.

However, Rosado didn't need details to show the impact that Sanchez left with those who knew him.

Sanchez's relatives and friends came to the homecoming Friday to hear the announcement of the David

Sanchez Memorial Award. From now on, the honor will be given each year to a student who exemplifies the spirit of Broughal, such as Sanchez had.

Ironically, Rosado's son played football this year for Broughal. One day after practice, the seventh-grader came home from school and told his father that jerseys were handed out. What number did you get, his father asked.

"I got number 32," the younger Rosado said.

"You got 32?"

Yes, the boy replied. The coach just gave him the jersey. It was the same number Sanchez wore.

"I could not believe the irony," Rosado told the students.

Soon, Rosado and Rotondo presented Sanchez's mother, Maria, with a No. 32 jersey.

Then, they announced the first winner of the award, Angel Torres, an eighth-grader. The solemn feeling lifted and students clapped and cheered as Torres took the stage.

Afterward, teens chatted loudly as they prepared for dismissal. Parents took more pictures of the homecoming court. People patted Rosado on the back and thanked him for a heart-warming program.

Maria Sanchez, slightly smiling and holding the yellow jersey, quietly slipped out the front door, back into the South Side.

Note: Shortly after the assembly, I located Maria Sanchez and I drove her home. She expressed her appreciation for the recognition and tribute we paid to her son David – she was very proud of him. Over the years, I would greet and speak with her when I saw her, usually at the supermarket. She was a private, independent and very religious lady.

Tragically, on September 25, 2006, Maria Sanchez was the victim of a gruesome attack. She was violently killed in her home – the same home where her son David was shot and killed twenty-seven years earlier. Like then, the community was outraged and deeply saddened.

I pray that they both rest in eternal peace.

A Closing Poem

A few years ago, while serving as assistant principal at Broughal Middle School, my students asked me to write a poem about myself to share with them and their parents during a written-words session at our family night. It's actually the only poem I've ever written.

I knew that the students had invested a lot of effort and feelings into their poems and I wanted to do the same. However, I didn't get to read my poem that night. It wasn't because I had reservations or was in any way hesitant. Because the activity was such a huge success, we had an overwhelming number of students sharing their poems, along with a few parents and teachers. We simply ran out of time.

It was probably for the best. I certainly did not want to deflect any attention away from the students and their willingness to express themselves honestly and openly. At the close of our family night, I put my poem in one of my desk drawers, where it remained until a few months before this book was complete. When I stumbled across it, I read it again for the first time in more than three years. At that moment, I immediately knew that I should use it in the book.

Who am I?

I'm a happy little boy who likes to play with his
friends. The hot summer days mean baseball and
swimming at Saucon Park pool.
At night we play hide and go seek, freeze tag and
kick the can.
During the fall, I walk to school with my friends.
We look forward to coming home to get together at
Clemente Park –
Where we will play until dark.
Snow, snow, snow – Ho, ho, ho.
Sled ridding, snowmen and snow ball fights –
Presents, great food and silent nights.
Life is good, life is fun, but the truth is – Life has not
yet begun.
I miss that little boy!

Who am I?

I'm a kid who has lost his innocence and is quickly
losing hope –
I'm surrounded by violence, poverty and dope.
Life is ugly and so am I.
Life hurts and it's getting worse.

My friends and I no longer get together to enjoy life,
but rather to escape it.
Other than anger, I had no feelings. I was numb -
At school most teachers believed I was dumb.
They either don't notice or don't care – That I am
hardly ever there.
When I do attend, it's not long before I'm in a fight.
It seems like it's all I do, fight, fight, fight –

Morning, noon and night.

As if life were not bad enough –
Now a dear friend was violently taken from us.
I still miss him!

Is this my life, rats and roaches, waiting for the welfare
check so that I might get a new pair of sneakers?
Waiting for the food stamps so that I could have milk
for my cereal?
I'm tired of waiting; I'm going to get mine –
Watch out world, here I come and I'm pissed!

How did I survive? I don't know.
Was it luck, was it a guardian angel or was it the ring?
Boxing – ding, ding, ding.
Left jab, right cross, left hook –
Black eyes and a broken nose, that's what it took.
Those that don't know may ask – how can that
brutality save you?
I say to them – the answer to life's questions are
within.

My rage now in remission – Could I succeed in life
from this position?
Although my anger was in check – My confidence
was still suspect.

College – who me, no way – what the heck – I was
not honors, I was not college prep.
I had to take some basic courses twice – I was from
flunker's paradise.
Lucky for me, someone believed in me more than
me – Off to college, yes indeed.

Livin' la vida loca I am. Classes, exams and parties –
Yes I can.

Meanwhile, back in the hood I'm misunderstood –
You a sellout, you acting white, keep it real.
You're just a poor Puerto Rican from the projects.

Reality check!

Who am I?

Am I fooling myself with college?
What happens if I try and don't succeed?
Reality check!
There has to be a life beyond the damned projects.

I'm going to pass on dealing drugs and the latest
hustle to get over on the system –
I'm now a college student, that's my new mission.

It's not easy for me and it got even tougher – Guess
what, we just had a baby.
If that weren't enough, I have no money and I have
to push my car to get it started.
Now I can quit, who would blame me?

I can make it, I just need a little help cleaning up this
mess –
I'll have a drink or two, it will ease the stress.
I'm numb again, not from anger, but from the poison
I ingest.

The next six years are a haze – I live my life in a maze.
The angel on my shoulder keeps me from self destruction –
But time is running out, I can barely function.
The time has come for me to deal with the true evils of life. Not the drugs, the violence, the poverty, but the forces within me that continue to lead me to self destruction.

The biggest challenge before me is me. I can beat anything the system throws at me, but I cannot continue to beat myself.
I have learned the secret to my success – life is full of obstacles, however the most difficult obstacles to overcome are those you place in front of yourself.

No longer do I doubt myself
No longer do I blame others
No longer do I see myself as a victim.

Who am I?

I'm a son, a brother and a father.
I'm a husband and a friend.
I'm a strong Puerto Rican man.

I'm a role model – not perfect – but a role model.
I'm a survivor for I have survived myself

Who am I?

I'm José Rosado, your assistant principal.

References

Foreword

1. 2003 National Youth Risk Behavior Survey
2. 2004 National Youth Gang Survey

Section I – I Feel Ya'

1. Sheldon B. Kopp, *If You Meet the Buddha on the Road, Kill Him! The Pilgrimage of Psychotherapy Patients*, (New York, NY, Bantam Doubleday Dell Publishing Group, Inc. 1971), p 7
2. Ibid., p. 189
3. Ibid., p. 21
4. Ibid., p. 40
5. Ibid., p. 40
6. Ibid., p. 146
7. Ibid., p. 81
8. Ibid., p. 83
9. Ibid., p. 83
10. Ibid., p. 136
11. Ibid., p. 193
12. Ibid., p. 109
13. Ibid., p. 99
14. Ibid., p. 105
15. Ibid., p. 25
16. Ibid., p. 224
17. Ibid., p. 128

Disclaimer: The Root of Evil

1. "Are Some Kids Born to be Bad?" by William McCall, The Associated Press, May 31, 1998.
2. Judith Rich Harris, *The Nurture Assumption: Why Children The Out the Way They Do*, (Free Press, A division of Simon & Schuster, Inc., New York, NY, Sept. 4, 1998).

Section II – Strike 1: Failure on the Home Front

1. "Fact Sheet on School-Age Children's Out-of-School Time," National Institute on Out-of-School Time, Center for Research on Women, Wellesley College, March 2001. Retrieved from http://www.niost.org
2. Ibid.
3. Ibid.
4. "2000 Annual Fifty State Survey," National Committee for the Prevention of Child Abuse (NCPCA). Retrieved from http://yesican.org/stats.html
5. Ibid.
6. "Prevent Child Abuse and Neglect, Statistics," New York City Administration for Children's Services, Retrieved from http://www.nyc.gov/html/getinvolved/abuseprevent_stats.html
7. Report of the American Psychological Association Presidential Task Force on Violence and the Family, APA, 1996. Retrieved from http://www.yesican.org/statisticsDV.html
8. "New Directions for Child Protective Services," Child Welfare Project, National Conference of State Legislatures. Retrieved from http://www.nosl.org/programs/cyf/cpsexsum.htm

9. "Suffer the Children," National Conference of State Legislatures. Retrieved from http://www.nosl.org/programs/pubs/bkchild.htm

10. "New Directions for Child Protective Services," Child Welfare Project, National Conference of State Legislatures. Retrieved from http://www.nosl.org/programs/cyf/cpsexsum.htm

11. Ibid.

12. "What Are You Going to Do About Child Abuse?" by Andrew Vachss, *Parade Magazine*, August 22, 2004.

13. "Prevent Child Abuse and Neglect, Statistics," New York City Administration for Children's Services. Retrieved from http://www.nyc.gov/html/acs/html/getinvolved/abuse prevent_stats.html

14. "Malignant Neglect: Substance Abuse and America's Schools," The National Center on Addiction and Substance Abuse at Columbia University, September 2001.

15. Statistics from the *Los Angeles Times*, September 19, 1988. Cited in Amneus, The Garbage Generation, page 179. Retrieved from http://www.divorcereform.org/crime.html

16. Ibid.

17. "A New Look at the Effects of Family Structure on Status Attainment," Social Science Quarterly 73 (1992): 581-595. Cited on page 72 of "The Abolition of Marriage," by Maggie Gallagher.

18. "Divorce Statistics: Our Online Quick Polls," Divorce Magazine.com. Retrieved from http://www.divorcemag.com/statistics/statsDM.shtml

19. "Malignant Neglect: Substance Abuse and America's Schools," The National Center on Addiction and Substance Abuse at Columbia University, September 2001.